THE DAY I STOPPED DRINKING MILK

Sudha Murty was born in 1950 in Shiggaon in north Karnataka. She did her MTech in computer science, and is now the chairperson of the Infosys Foundation. A prolific writer in English and Kannada, she has written novels, technical books, travelogues, collections of short stories and non-fiction pieces, and four books for children. Her books have been translated into all the major Indian languages.

Sudha Murty was the recipient of the R.K. Narayan Award for Literature and the Padma Shri in 2006, and the Attimabbe Award from the government of Karnataka for excellence in Kannada literature in 2011.

Also by the same author

SUDHA MURTY

THE DAY I STOPPED DRINKING MILK

Life Stories from Here and There

PENGUIN BOOKS

PENGUIN BOOKS
Published by the Penguin Group
Penguin Books India Pvt. Ltd, 7th Floor, Infinity Tower C, DLF Cyber City,
Gurgaon 122 002, Haryana, India
Penguin Group (USA) Inc., 375 Hudson Street, New York, New York 10014, USA
Penguin Group (Canada), 90 Eglinton Avenue East, Suite 700, Toronto, Ontario,
M4P 2Y3, Canada
Penguin Books Ltd, 80 Strand, London WC2R 0RL, England
Penguin Ireland, 25 St Stephen's Green, Dublin 2, Ireland (a division of Penguin
Books Ltd)
Penguin Group (Australia), 707 Collins Street, Melbourne, Victoria 3008, Australia
Penguin Group (NZ), 67 Apollo Drive, Rosedale, Auckland 0632, New Zealand
Penguin Books (South Africa) (Pty) Ltd, Block D, Rosebank Office Park, 181 Jan
Smuts Avenue, Parktown North, Johannesburg 2193, South Africa

Penguin Books Ltd, Registered Offices: 80 Strand, London WC2R 0RL, England

First published by Penguin Books India 2012

Copyright © Sudha Murty 2012

16 15 14 13 12

ISBN 9780143418658

Typeset in Dante MT by Eleven Arts, Delhi
Printed at Repro India Ltd, Navi Mumbai

A PENGUIN RANDOM HOUSE COMPANY

*To Lakshmi, my new daughter
and Rishi, my new son*

Contents

Preface

One may wonder why I am writing about the personal lives of many people who have confided in me about their problems. Isn't it unethical to do so? However, most of the people I have written about requested me to change their names and use their problems as case studies. Some like Vishnu and Portado encouraged me to tell their stories so that others should not become like them. I thank all these people wholeheartedly and am grateful for their strength and kindness that has allowed me to share their stories with you.

This is my fourth book of recollections of my experiences as a teacher, a writer and a social worker. I want to thank my new editor, Shrutkeerti Khurana, whose hard work has made an immense difference to this book. Her constant interaction with me made me think of some stories in a different way and also helped me look at things from a youngster's point of view.

I would also like to thank Udayan Mitra of Penguin Books for convincing me to bring out a new volume of my stories and thoughts.

SUDHA MURTY

1

Bombay to Bangalore

It was the beginning of summer. I was boarding Udyan Express at Gulbarga railway station. My destination was Bangalore. As I boarded the train, I saw that the second-class compartment was jam-packed with people. Though the compartment was reserved, there were many unauthorized people in it. This side of Karnataka is popularly known as Hyderabad Karnataka since the Nizam of Hyderabad once ruled this area. There is scarcity of water here, which makes the land dry, and the farmers cannot grow anything during summer. Hence, many poor farmers and landless labourers from Hyderabad Karnataka immigrate to Bangalore and other big cities during the summer for jobs in construction. They return to their homes in the rainy season to cultivate their lands. This was April, so the train compartment was particularly crowded.

I sat down and was pushed to the corner of the berth. Though it was meant for three people, there were already six of us sitting on it. I looked around and saw students who were eager to come to Bangalore and explore different options to enhance their careers. There were merchants who were talking about what goods to order from Bangalore. Some government officers, though, were criticizing Gulbarga. 'What a place! Staying here is impossible because of the heat. No wonder people call this a punishment transfer!'

The ticket collector came in and started checking people's tickets and reservations. It was difficult to guess who had a ticket and who had a reservation. Some people had tickets but no reservation. This was an overnight train and people needed sleeper berths, but they were limited in number. People who did not have a reserved berth were begging the ticket collector to accommodate them 'somehow'. It was next to impossible for him to listen to everyone.

With his eagle eye, he easily located people who did not have a ticket. People without tickets were pleading, 'Sir, the previous train was cancelled. We had a reservation on that train. It is not our fault. We don't want to pay for this ticket again.' Some were begging him, 'Sir, I was late to the station and there was a big queue. I didn't have time to buy a ticket. So, I got into this compartment.' The collector must have read the Bhagavad Gita thoroughly; he remained calm while listening to their stories and kept issuing new tickets for ticketless passengers.

Suddenly, he looked in my direction and asked, 'What about your ticket?'

'I have already shown my ticket to you,' I said.

'Not you, madam, the girl hiding below your berth. Hey, come out, where is your ticket?'

I realized that someone was sitting below my berth. When the collector yelled at her, the girl came out of hiding. She was thin, dark, scared and looked like she had been crying profusely. She must have been about thirteen or fourteen years old. She had uncombed hair and was dressed in a torn skirt and blouse. She was trembling and folded both her hands.

The collector asked again, 'Who are you? From which station did you get on? Where are you going? I can issue a full ticket for you with a fine.'

The girl did not reply. The collector was getting very angry since he had been dealing with countless ticketless passengers. He took out his anger on this little girl. 'I know all you runaways,' he shouted. 'You take a free ride in trains and cause tremendous problems. You neither reply to my questions nor pay for your ticket. I have to answer to my bosses . . .'

The girl still did not say anything. The people around the girl were not bothered at all and went about their business. Some were counting the money for their ticket and some were getting ready to get down at Wadi Junction, the next stop. People on the top berth were preparing to sleep and others were busy with their dinner. This was something unusual for me, because I had never seen such a situation in my vast experience of social work.

The girl stood quietly as if she had not heard anything. The collector caught hold of her arms and told her to get down at the next station. 'I will hand you over to the police myself. They will put you in an orphanage,' he said. 'It is not my headache. Get down at Wadi.'

The girl did not move. The collector started forcibly pulling her out from the compartment. Suddenly, I had a strange feeling. I stood up and called out to the collector. 'Sir, I will pay for her ticket,' I said. 'It is getting dark. I don't want a young girl on the platform at this time.'

The collector raised his eyebrows and looked at me. He smiled and said, 'Madam, it is very kind of you to offer to buy her a ticket. But I have seen many children like her. They get in at one station, then get off at the next and board another train. They beg or travel to their destination without a ticket. This is not an exceptional case. Why do you want to waste your money? She will not travel even with a ticket. She may leave if you just give her some money.'

I looked out of the compartment. The train was approaching Wadi Junction and the platform lights were bright. Vendors of tea, juice and food were running towards the train. It was dark. My heart did not accept the collector's advice—and I always listen to my heart. What the collector said might be true but what would I lose—just a few hundred rupees?

'Sir, that's fine. I will pay for her ticket anyway,' I said.

I asked the girl, 'Will you tell me where you want to go?'

The girl looked at me with disbelief. It was at this moment that I noticed her beautiful, dark eyes, which were grief-stricken. She did not say a word.

The collector smiled and said, 'I told you, madam. Experience is the best teacher.'

He turned to the girl and said, 'Get down.'

Then he looked at me and said, 'Madam, if you give her ten rupees, she will be much happier with that than with the ticket.'

I did not listen to him. I told the collector to give me

a ticket to the last destination, Bangalore, so that the girl could get down wherever she wanted.

The collector looked at me again and said, 'But she won't get a berth and you will have to pay a penalty.'

I quietly opened my purse.

The collector continued, 'If you want to pay, then you should pay for the ticket from the train's starting point.'

The train originated from Bombay VT and terminated at Bangalore. I paid up quietly. The collector issued the ticket and left in disdain.

The girl was left standing in the same position. I asked my fellow passengers to move and give the girl some space to sit down because she now held a valid ticket. They moved very reluctantly. Then, I asked the girl to sit on the seat—but she did not. When I insisted, she sat down on the floor.

I did not know where to start the conversation. I ordered a meal for her and when the dinner box came, she held it in her hands but did not eat. I failed to persuade her to eat or talk. Finally, I gave the ticket to her and said, 'Look, I don't know what's on your mind since you refuse to talk to me. So, here's the ticket. You can get down wherever you want to.'

As the night progressed, people started sleeping on the floor and on their berths, but the girl continued to sit.

When I woke up at six o'clock the next morning, she was dozing. That meant that she had not got down anywhere. Her dinner box was empty and I was happy that she had at least eaten something.

As the train approached Bangalore, the compartment started getting empty. Again, I told her to sit on the seat and this time she obliged. Slowly, she started talking. She told me that her name was Chitra. She lived in a village near Bidar. Her father was a coolie and she had lost her mother at birth. Her father had remarried and had two sons with her stepmother. But a few months ago, her father had died. Her stepmother started beating her often and did not give her food. I knew from her torn, bloodstained blouse and the marks on her body that she was telling the truth. She was tired of that life. She did not have anybody to support her so she left home in search of something better.

By this time, the train had reached Bangalore. I said goodbye to Chitra and got down from the train. My driver came and picked up my bags. I felt someone watching me. When I turned back, Chitra was standing there and looking at me with sad eyes. But there was nothing more that I could do.

As I started walking towards my car, I realized that Chitra was following me. I knew that she did not have anybody in the whole world. Now, I was at a loss. I did not know what to do with her. I had paid her ticket out of compassion but I had never thought that she was going to be my responsibility! But from Chitra's perspective, I had been kind to her and she wanted to cling on to me. When I got into the car, she stood outside watching me.

I was scared for a minute. 'What am I doing?' I questioned myself. I was worried about the safety of a girl in Wadi Junction station, but now I was leaving her in a big city like Bangalore—a situation worse than the previous one. Anything could happen to Chitra here. After all, she was a girl. There were many ways in which people could exploit her situation.

I told her to get into my car. My driver looked at the girl curiously. I told him to take us to my friend Ram's place. Ram ran separate shelter homes for boys and girls. We at the Infosys Foundation supported him financially on a regular basis. I thought Chitra could stay there for some time and we could talk about her future after I came back from my tours in a few weeks. There were about ten girls in the shelter and three of them were of Chitra's age. Most of the girls there already knew me.

As soon as I reached the shelter, the lady supervisor came out to talk to me. I explained the situation and handed Chitra over to her. I told Chitra, 'You can stay here for two weeks. Don't worry. These are very good people. I will come and see you after two weeks. Don't run away from here, at least until I come back. Talk to your lady supervisor. You can call her Akka.' (Akka means elder sister in the Kannada language.) I handed over some money to the supervisor and told her to buy some clothes and other necessary things for the girl.

After two weeks, I went back to the shelter. I was not sure if Chitra would even be there. But to my surprise, I saw Chitra looking much happier than before. She was having good food for the first time in her life. She was wearing new clothes and was teaching lessons to the younger children. As soon as she saw me, she stood up eagerly. The supervisor said, 'Chitra is a nice girl. She helps in our kitchen, cleans the shelter and also teaches the younger children. She tells us that she was a good student in her village and wanted to join high school but her family didn't allow her to do so. Here, she is comfortable and wants to study further. What are your plans for her future? Can we keep her here?'

Soon, Ram also joined us. Ram knew the whole story and suggested that Chitra could go to a high school nearby. I immediately agreed and said that I would sponsor her expenses as long as she continued to study.

I left the shelter knowing that Chitra had found a home and a new direction in her life.

I got busier with my work and my visits to the shelter reduced to once a year. But I always inquired about Chitra's well-being over the phone. I knew that she was studying well and that her progress was good.

Years went by. One day, Ram phoned me and said that Chitra had scored 85 per cent in her tenth class. When I went to the shelter to congratulate and talk to her, she was very happy. She was growing up to be a confident young woman. There was brightness in her beautiful, dark eyes.

I offered to sponsor her college studies if she wanted to continue studying. But she said, 'No, Akka. I have talked to my friends and made up my mind. I would like to do my diploma in computer science so that I can immediately get a job after three years.' I tried to persuade her to go to college for a bachelor's degree in engineering but she did not agree. She wanted to become economically independent as soon as possible. Somewhere inside me, I understood where she was coming from.

Three rainy seasons passed. Chitra obtained her diploma with flying colours. She also got a job in a software company as an assistant testing engineer. When she got her first salary, she came to my office with a sari and a box of sweets. I was touched by her gesture. Later, I got to know that she had spent her entire first salary buying something for everyone at the shelter.

Soon enough, Ram called me to discuss a new problem. 'Chitra is now a working girl. So she cannot stay in the shelter since it is only meant for students.' I told Ram that I would talk to Chitra and ask her to pay the shelter a reasonable amount of money per month towards rent. This way she could continue to stay there until she got married. I strongly felt that the shelter was a safe place for an unmarried, orphan girl like Chitra.

Ram asked me, 'Are you going to look for a boy for her?'

This was a new and an even bigger problem. As her informal guardian, I had to find a boy for Chitra or she herself had to find a life partner. This was a great responsibility. No wonder people say I have a penchant for getting into problems! But God also shows me unique ways of getting out of them. I told Ram, 'She is only twenty-one. Let her work for a few years. If you come across a suitable boy, please let me know.'

I called Chitra and gave her my opinion about staying at the shelter, and she happily agreed to stay on and pay rent.

Days rolled by, and months turned into years. One day, when I was in Delhi, I got a call from Chitra. She was very happy. 'Akka, my company is sending me to the USA! I wanted to meet you and take your blessings but you are not here in Bangalore.'

I was ecstatic for Chitra. I said, 'Chitra, you are now going to a different country. Take care of yourself and keep in touch. My blessings are always with you.'

Years passed. Occasionally, I received an email from Chitra. She was doing very well in her career. She was posted across several cities in USA and was enjoying life. I silently prayed that she should always be happy wherever she was.

Years later, I was invited to deliver a lecture in San Francisco for Kannada Koota, an organization where families who speak Kannada meet and organize events. The lecture was in a convention hall of a hotel and I decided to stay at the same hotel. After the lecture, I was planning to leave for the airport. When I checked out of the hotel room and went to the reception counter to pay the bill, the receptionist said, 'Ma'am, you don't need to pay us anything. The lady over there has already settled your bill. She must know you pretty well.'

I turned around and found Chitra there. She was standing with a young white man and wore a beautiful sari. She was looking very pretty with short hair. Her dark eyes were beaming with happiness and pride. As soon as she saw me, she gave me a brilliant smile, hugged me and touched my feet. I was overwhelmed with joy and did not know what to say.

'Chitra, how are you? I have not seen you since ages. What a sweet surprise. How did you know that I will be in this city today?'

'Akka, I live in this city and came to know that you are giving a lecture at the local Kannada Koota. I am also a member there. I wanted to surprise you. It is not difficult to find out about your schedule.'

'Chitra, I have so many questions to ask you. How is work? Have you visited India? And more importantly, have you found Mr Right? And why did you pay my hotel bill?'

'No, Akka. I haven't come to India since I left. If I come to India, how can I return here without meeting you? Akka, I have something to tell you. I know that you were always worried about my marriage. You never asked me about my community. But you always wanted me to settle down. I know it is hard for you to choose a boy for me. Now, I have found my Mr Right. Please meet my colleague, John. We are getting married at the end of the year. You must come for our wedding and bless us.'

I was very happy to see the way things had turned out for Chitra. But I came back to my original question.

'Chitra, why did you pay my hotel bill? That is not right.'

With tears in her eyes and gratitude on her face, she said, 'Akka, if you hadn't helped me, I don't know where I would have been today—maybe a beggar, a prostitute, a runaway child, a servant in someone's house . . . or I may even have committed suicide. You changed my life. I am ever grateful to you.'

'No, Chitra. I am only one step in your ladder of success,' I said. 'There are many steps which led you to where you are today—the shelter which looked after you, the schools which gave you good education, the company which sent you to America and, above all, it is you—the most determined and inspired girl who made your life yourself. One step should never take the credit for the end result.'

'That is your thinking, Akka. I differ with you,' she said.

'Chitra, you are starting a new life and you should save money for your new family. Why did you pay my hotel bill?'

Chitra did not reply but told John to touch my feet. Then, suddenly sobbing, she hugged me and said, 'Because you paid for my ticket from Bombay to Bangalore!'

2

Rahman's Avva

Rahman was a young and soft-spoken employee who worked in a BPO. He was also an active volunteer in our Foundation. He would not talk without reason and would never boast about his achievements.

Rahman was a perfectionist. So any assignment given to him was done exceedingly well. He worked for the Foundation on the weekends and was very kind to the children in the orphanage. He spent his own money and always brought sweets for the children. I really liked him.

Since we worked closely together, he learnt that I am from North Karnataka, from Dharwad district. My language has that area's accent and my love for Dharwad food is very well known. One day, Rahman came and asked me, 'Ma'am, if you are free this Sunday, will you come to my house? My mother and sister are visiting me. Incidentally, my mother is also from Dharwad district. My family has read your columns in Kannada and your books too. When I told them that I am working with you, they expressed their earnest desire to meet you. Is it possible for you to have lunch with us?'

'Will you assure me that I'll get a good Dharwad meal?' I joked.

'I assure you, ma'am. My mother is a great cook.'

'Come on, Rahman. Every boy gives this compliment to his mother, however bad she may be at cooking. It is the mother's love that makes the food great.'

'No, she really is an amazing cook. Even my wife says so.'

'Then she must be really great because no daughter-in-law praises her mother-in-law's cooking without merit,' I smiled. 'By the way, which village in Dharwad district do they come from?'

He told me the name of a village near Ranebennur that I had never heard of. I happily agreed to visit them for lunch.

That Sunday, I took some flowers along. Rahman's newly constructed apartment was on Bannerghatta Road near the zoo. When I entered his home, I met his wife Salma. She was a smart and good-looking girl. She worked as a teacher in the kindergarten nearby.

Then, he called out to his Avva. A mother is usually

referred to as Avva in North Karnataka. An old lady with grey hair came out of the kitchen. Rahman introduced her, 'This is my mother.' I was a bit surprised—she was not quite what I had expected. She was wearing a huge bindi the size of a 25-paise coin and an Ilkal sari with lots of green bangles on both arms. She kept the sari pallu on her head. She had a contented smile on her face and with folded hands she said, 'Namaste.'

Rahman's sister entered from another room. She was so different from Rahman. Rahman was fair and very handsome. His sister was tall and dark. She was wearing a cotton sari with a smaller bindi than her mother and also had two gold bangles on her hands. Rahman said, 'This is my sister Usha. She stays in Hirekerur. Both her husband and she are school teachers.'

I felt confused after meeting Rahman's mother and sister but I did not ask any questions.

After I sat down comfortably, Usha said, 'Madam, we love your stories because we feel connected to them. I teach some of your children's stories at school.'

Salma also joined the conversation. 'Even I like them, but my students are too young to understand.'

Rahman smiled and said, 'You must be surprised to see my mother and sister. I want to share my story with you.'

His mother went back to the kitchen and Usha started cleaning the table. Salma went to help her mother-in-law. Only the two of us remained.

'Ma'am, you must be wondering why my mother and sister are Hindus while I am a Muslim. Only you can understand and appreciate my life story because I have seen you helping people from all religions and communities without bias. I remember your comment to me: we can't choose the community or religion that we are born into—so we should never think that our community is our identity.'

Rahman paused, then continued, 'Ma'am, I believe in that too because I have also been brought up that way. I want to share my life and my perspective with you.'

Rahman started his story.

'Thirty years ago, Kashibai and Datturam lived in the outskirts of our village with their six-month-old daughter Usha. They looked after the ten-acre field of their landlord, Srikant Desai, who lived in Bombay. Srikant only came once a year to collect the revenue. The field was very large and it was too much for Kashibai and Datturam to handle. So, they requested the landlord to get another family to stay with them and help with the field. They also welcomed the thought of having company.

'Srikant contacted his acquaintances and found a

suitable family. Soon, Fatima Bi and Husain Saab came to the village. They occupied one portion of the house and the other portion stayed with Kashibai and Datturam. Husain Saab and Datturam got along very well. However, Kashibai and Fatima Bi didn't see eye to eye at all. It is not that they were bad women but their nature were very different. Kashibai was loud, very frank and hard-working. Fatima Bi was quiet, lazy and an introvert. Inevitably, there was a fight. It all started with a hen. Kashibai's hen would come to Fatima Bi's portion of the house and lay eggs. Fatima Bi wouldn't return the eggs because she thought that her hen had laid them. Kashibai even tried colouring her hen to distinguish it from Fatima Bi's. Both the ladies shared a common well and would fight because both wanted to wash their vessels and clothes almost always at the same time. They also fought about their goats. Fatima Bi's goats came and ate Kashibai's flowers and leaves, which she used for her puja. Sometimes, Kashibai's goats went to Fatima Bi's place and left their droppings behind. Fatima Bi wouldn't return the droppings either.'

'What's so great about droppings?' I interrupted.

'Ma'am, goat droppings are used as manure.'

'Oh, I understand. Please continue,' I urged Rahman.

'The fights continued and sometimes Kashibai felt that she had made a mistake to tell their landlord that they wanted neighbours. She felt that she had been very happy without Fatima Bi. Fatima Bi also wanted to leave the farm and go to some other village but Husain Saab didn't agree. He would say, "You women fight about unnecessary things. This is a good opportunity for us to make money. The land is fertile and there is plenty of water. Our landlord is good and hardly visits. We can easily grow vegetables. Where can I get such work nearby? You should also become active like Kashibai and drop your ego. Try to adjust with her." The same conversation would happen on the other side of the house. Datturam would tell his wife, "Don't be so aggressive. You should mellow down like Fatima. Though she is lazy, she is good-natured."

'But as usual, both women never listened to their husbands.

'As time went by, Kashibai's daughter Usha turned two years old. Fatima Bi loved children and enjoyed seeing Usha play in the field. Fatima Bi liked henna a lot. Every month, she coloured her hand with henna from the plant in the field and Usha always joined her. Usha was fascinated with the beautiful orange colour. She would come home and tell her mother, "Why can't you also colour your hand like Fatima Kaku?" (Kaku is equivalent to 'aunt' in the local language.)

'This comment irritated Kashibai. She said, "Fatima can afford to colour her hands because her husband works and also helps in the kitchen. She sits on the bed and listens to the radio. If I do that, will your father come and work in the kitchen?" Fatima Bi would overhear their conversation but still she continued her friendship with little Usha.

'When Fatima became pregnant, she became even lazier. She eventually reached full term and a distant relative came to help Fatima with her delivery. A few days later, there was a festival in the village and Datturam and his family went to attend it. When they came back, Fatima Bi was not there. She was already in the hospital in critical condition and had delivered a son. The house was in complete silence. But the silence was deafening to Kashibai's ears. She started crying. She was very sad because Fatima Bi was in the hospital in such a serious condition. The next day, they learnt that Fatima Bi was no more.

'Husain Saab was left with his newborn son. The midwife stayed for a month and left. It was an uphill task for Husain Saab to look after a small baby. Neither Husain Saab nor Fatima Bi had any relatives who could take care of the little one. Most of them were coolies and a newborn child would only be a burden to the relatives.

Datturam was very sympathetic and allowed Husain Saab to work less in the field but taking care of a small baby alone is very difficult.

'One night, the child started crying non-stop and Kashibai could not take it. She felt that enough was enough. After all, it was a little baby. A woman is so different from a man when it comes to rearing a child. Her motherly instinct made her go next door and tap on Husain Saab's door without even waiting for her husband. When Husain Saab opened the door, she told him, "Husain Saab, give me the baby. I am a mother. I know how to handle him." She picked up the baby boy, held him in her pallu and brought him to her house holding him tightly to her chest. The baby boy stopped crying immediately. For the first time since the baby was born, Husain Saab slept through the night comfortably.

'The next day, Kashibai told Husain Saab, "I will look after this child until you get married again. Don't worry." She forgot her enmity with Fatima Bi and even felt ashamed. She thought that she should have been nicer to Fatima Bi. Now, Kashibai did not even bother about where the droppings of the goats fell or where the hens laid their eggs. For her, looking after the baby was more important.

'The baby was named Rahman and, to everyone's surprise, Husain Saab did not remarry. Rahman grew up in Kashibai's house and started calling her Avva and Usha became his Akka. Rahman continued to sleep in his father's house but as soon as the sun rose, he ran to Kashibai's house to get ready. While Usha bathed on her own, Kashibai bathed little Rahman. She gave them breakfast, packed their lunches and walked them to school. Though Usha was two years older than Rahman, Kashibai made sure that they studied in the same class. Kashibai worked in the field in the afternoon and brought the children back in the evenings. Husain Saab cooked Rahman's dinner and Rahman would go back and sleep with his father at night. This continued for ten years.

'When Rahman was ten and Usha was twelve years old, Husain Saab fell ill and all his savings were spent on his treatment. Meanwhile, Kashibai purchased two she-buffaloes and started a milk business. She started earning more money than her husband.

'That same year, Husain Saab died of tuberculosis. Rahman was left all alone. There were hardly any people at Husain Saab's burial. A distant uncle came and told the mullah that he would take care of Rahman. But when the time came to take Rahman away, the uncle did not turn up at all. Without a second thought, Datturam and Kashibai took him in. Rahman was happy to stay in Kashibai's house.

'Kashibai was very conscious about Rahman's religion. Every Friday, she sent him for namaaz and on holidays she sent him for Koran class at the local mosque. She told him to participate in all Muslim festivals even though there were very few Muslims in the village. Rahman also took part in the Hindu festivals celebrated in his house. Datturam and Kashibai bought two cycles for both the kids. Rahman and Usha cycled to high school and later they also rode their cycles to the same college.

'Eventually, they graduated and that day Kashibai told Rahman, "Unfortunately, we don't have a picture of your parents. So, turn towards Mecca and pray to Allah. Pray to Fatima Bi and Husain Saab. They will bless you. You are now grown up and independent. Usha is getting married next month. My responsibility to both Usha and you is now over."

'Kashibai's affection and devotion overwhelmed Rahman, who could not remember his own mother's face. He prayed to Allah and his parents and then touched Kashibai's feet. He said, "Avva, you are my Ammi. You are my Mecca."

'Rahman got a job in a BPO in Bangalore and left home. He worked for different firms for a few years, grew in his career and started earning a good salary. He met Salma at a friend's wedding and fell in love with her.

After getting Kashibai and Datturam's approval, he got married to Salma.'

When he finished his story, Rahman was very emotional and in tears.

I was amazed at Kashibai. She was uneducated but far advanced in human values. I was surprised and humbled by the largeness of her heart. Kashibai had raised the boy with his own religion and still loved him like her son.

By this time, lunch was ready and Usha invited me to eat. While having the delicious lunch, I asked Usha, 'What made you decide to visit here?'

'I have holidays at school and I took an extended vacation so I could come for Panchami.'

Panchami is a festival celebrated mostly by girls, particularly married women, who come to their brother's house. It is similar to the Rakhi festival in the north, where a brother acknowledges his sister's love. I recalled our history and remembered that Queen Karunavati had sent a rakhi to Emperor Humayun seeking his protection.

Now, I looked at the wall in the dining room and for the first time I noticed two pictures in Rahman's house, one of Mecca and the other of Krishna, both hanging side by side.

3

Ganga's Ghat

Ganga was a coolie in a tiny village in Karnataka which is infamous for droughts. She was a middle-aged woman who lived in a thatched hut near the rocks; she never locked her hut because there was nothing to steal from it. Her routine was simple. She got up in the morning, went to the fields to work, earned her daily wage and then came back home to fetch water, have a bath, cook her meal, eat and sleep. Her routine was the same on all days except Mondays, which was a village holiday.

Normally, everything was closed in the village on Monday because it is the day of Lord Ishwara and Nandi is his vehicle. So Monday was considered to be a rest day for the bullocks and a holiday for the village.

Water was a big problem in the village because of the rocks around the area. The government had dug borewells, and water was stored in a tank. Everybody had to walk half a kilometre to fetch water from the tank. However, in the summer, it was very hard to get water because there was no electricity and the muddy road would get very hot. Hence, summer was a curse to the people in the village.

Ganga used to feel useless at home. She was very lonely and did not know what to do on the days when she did not have work. During the summer, she did not get much work anyway because of the limited work available in the fields. She felt depressed knowing that she had no aim in life and nothing to live for.

One hot summer evening, she came back from the fields after work and felt very tired. She had her bath and was just about to start cooking when she saw an old beggar standing in front of her hut.

Ganga said, 'Old man, I haven't cooked yet, and I have very little rice today. You can come another day and I will give you some food.'

The old man did not answer. Ganga repeated herself. Then, he said, 'Akka, I do not want rice. Can you give me one bucket of lukewarm water? My body is itchy. Someone said that I should take a bath in lukewarm water. That will reduce the itching. I am unable to sleep at night. In the summer, there is a lot of dust and it is affecting me in this old age.'

Ganga was very upset at his strange request. She said, 'It is not easy to get water in this village. In the hot summer, I have to walk half a kilometre to get water. I can't do this job for you.'

'Akka, I don't have anybody. Neither do I have vessels or firewood. After all, I am a beggar. You are so well-off. You have a hut to stay, vessels, firewood and water. If you don't give me water, I will go away,' he said.

As he turned to leave, Ganga had an indescribable feeling. Nobody had ever told her that she was a rich woman. Nobody had ever called her Akka or asked her for anything. She was always ordered around at work. This was an unusual feeling and she liked it. She changed her mind and called out to the beggar, 'Old man, sit down. I will give you a bucket of lukewarm water.'

When she gave the water, she saw that he was happy. He took a bath on the side of her hut and rubbed his body with a stone instead of soap. He was careful while using the water. After he finished his bath, he changed to another set of torn clothes and said, 'Akka, God bless you.' Then he went away.

The next day, as Ganga was about to start cooking, the beggar came again. Just looking at him irritated her. She thought that once you help a beggar, they never leave you. They know how to get what they want by sheer perseverance.

She was a little rude this time: 'Why have you come again?'

'Akka, I slept very well last night. I have come again to beg you for another bucket of lukewarm water.'

Ganga did not answer. Her mind said no but her heart said yes. What was she going to lose? Just a bucket of water. The old man patiently waited for her answer. She looked at her vessel. There were three buckets of water stored in it. Without saying anything, she heated the water and gave him a bucket. He took a bath, blessed her and went his way.

The following day, she knew that he might come again. So she fetched an extra bucket of water. As usual, he appeared again. Before he could even say anything, Ganga handed him a bucket of lukewarm water and said, 'Don't repeat this again. I can't do this every day.'

'Akka, if you can give me water for a week, I will be very grateful. I am old and can't bring water but I can get dry leaves from the forest for you. They may help you in cooking.' The old man had his bath and left.

As promised, he brought a bundle of dry leaves for Ganga the next day. Ganga knew that he would come for a week. So she always got extra water. Now, every morning, she got up with a purpose. She had to fetch more water. Though it was tiresome, she had a goal. Someone waited for her. Someone blessed her every day. It was a good feeling.

After a week, she thought that the old man might not come again. But on that day, she saw two people coming towards her hut. The old man had brought another old beggar, who was in an equally shabby condition and kept scratching his body. Ganga knew what was coming next. Before they could ask, she said, 'This is not a bathing ghat. You can't bring people here and expect me to keep giving water for their baths.'

Both of them stood silently and did not move. Then the first old man said, 'Please give us some water, Akka. He is really unwell. If you give us one bucket, we will share it somehow.'

Ganga knew that they would not leave unless she gave them water. Grumbling, she gave them one and a half buckets of water. They thanked her profusely and shared the water so carefully that not a drop was wasted. Ganga wanted to tell them, 'Next time, you get your own bucket of water and I will warm it.' But she was unable to say so looking at their condition and old age.

The next day, she was plucking mangoes from the

mango fields at work, and she knew that two people would come to her hut today. She was wondering how she would manage to make an extra trip to the tank to get water.

Her colleague Yamuna asked her, 'Why are you looking so worried, Ganga? The crop is good. We will continue to get work. The coolie rate is also high. You don't have too much expense either. You should be happy.'

Ganga then explained her problem. Yamuna smiled and said, 'Look, if you really want to give them water, I will help you. My eldest son brings water on his cycle. I will request him to give one pot of water to you every day and leave it outside your hut.'

Thus, Ganga's problem was solved.

Now, Ganga started giving two buckets of water to the two old men every day. After ten days, she saw three people in the line. But this time, she did not get upset. She knew that word had spread. People knew that if you want to have a bath, you should go to Ganga's place. She thought, 'What is wrong in giving water? It may be extra work for me, but at least some people benefit from it. What do I do after cooking anyway? I just go to bed. If I work for another half hour, some people might feel better and will even bless me.' This time, without their asking, she gave them three buckets of water.

She was right. Word had spread in the village that Ganga gave free water, warmed, to people for a bath. Some beneficiaries were able-bodied, middle-aged men. They fetched water for her. In the village, some people thought that they themselves could not do this service, so they decided to donate a bucket of water to Ganga every day.

Now, Ganga found that she did not have vessels to store so much water. Almost immediately, a kind-hearted philanthropist gave her a big drum. Also, whoever went to fetch firewood from the forest started dropping a small bundle in front of her hut so that she could use it to heat water.

Ganga never asked anyone why he or she was bringing water to her or keeping firewood on her doorstep. She did her work without talking.

A few months later, women also joined the queue. Ganga made a separate bathing area with walls made out of coconut leaves for the women. She continued her work as a coolie during the day and did this work in the evenings. Now, the number of people gradually increased to thirty and eventually it reached forty.

The season changed. The rains began and it started getting cool. Now, Ganga had to provide hot water for the baths.

Ganga had found her mission in life. She got up in the mornings and went to work. After she came back in the evenings, she checked the quantity of water. If there was not enough water, she fetched some more. Firewood was never a problem and was always in excess.

When I met Ganga, I was taken aback by what she was doing. She never got any public recognition but she was very clear that she did not want to talk to the media. She said, 'I do this because I love it. This gave me an opportunity to serve people like me who don't have anything in life. One needn't have much money to help people. I don't spend any money on this. In a dusty place like this, skin diseases are common. A bath a day keeps the skin doctor away.' And she smiled at her own attempt at humour.

With my overenthusiasm, I said, 'Ganga, I will give you a box of soaps and a hundred cotton towels. You can gift this to everybody. Our medicinal soap might even help them.'

I thought that she would jump for joy but she did not. She said, 'Madam, even today, I don't lock my hut. People are aware of my work and they help me on their own. The moment you give me soap and towels, I will have to keep them under lock and key. Once I distribute the soap, which is perishable, people will ask me for more. Some people may even ask me for a different brand of soap. Once the towel is torn, they will ask me for a new one. If I don't give them, people will think that I hide soaps and towels. I want to do this work within my own limits. If you want to give them soaps and towels, you can give it to the people yourself. I don't have any objection.'

I realized Ganga's philosophy and accepted it wholeheartedly. I knew that she was right. Money comes with expectations and spoils the delicate equilibrium of social work.

Suddenly, I was reminded of the river Ganga. The river flows from the Himalayas and we believe that, if we take a dip in her, it will wash away all our sins and diseases. Hence, the bathing ghats at Varanasi, Hardwar and Rishikesh are famous. I felt peaceful and thought that this Ganga's bathing ghat was no less than the bathing ghats of the river Ganga.

4

The Day I Stopped Drinking Milk

The state of Odisha is beautiful. It has blue mountains known as Niladri, beautiful rivers like Mahanadi, and enchanting forests. It is famous for its historical places like Udayagiri, Dhauli, the largest saltwater lake, Chilka, and the famous Rath Yatra of Jagannath at Puri. Nobody can forget the war of Kalinga, which took place on the banks of Daya River. Even today, when you visit Ashoka's inscription on the rock edict, you realize the greatness of Kalinga, or today's Odisha. But with all these natural resources, there is also a darker side to the state—the poor and tribal people of Odisha.

I was working in a remote village and we were building a school for children there. The area had a beautiful mountain and a lake and there was greenery everywhere. The inaccessible road to the village helped retain its beauty. One day, I was in the village for work and it started raining heavily. When it pours, it is very difficult to get out of the forest and it is impossible to know how long the rains might last. I had a translator with me who knew both Oriya and English and he was helping me in my work. He suggested that we take shelter in a hut nearby until the rain stopped. So we went to the nearest hamlet of huts.

The hut was small and had a thatched roof and mud flooring. As we entered, I noticed that it was a single large room partitioned into two. The first portion doubled as a hall during the day and a bedroom at night. The second portion was the kitchen. The owner of the hut came and welcomed us in. He gave us a mat to sit on. I saw that the pouring rain and the gushing water were joining the lake in front of the hut. It was a riveting moment. Even though I heard my watch ticking, I felt that time was standing still. The owner's baby boy was crying inside and his mother was singing a lullaby to soothe him. After some time, my translator got bored and told me that he was going out and would join me after an hour or so. I asked him where he was planning to go in this pouring rain. He told me that he was going to a small shop near the hut.

My host wanted to give me something to eat or drink. Indian hospitality dictates that if any guest comes to your house, you must offer them something, no matter how poor you are. The Taittiriya Upanishad says, '*Athiti devo bhava.*' This means that God comes home in the form of a guest. Indians believe that you must serve your guest, going out of your way if necessary. This man was no exception.

He did not speak my language, so he asked me in his broken Hindi, 'Tea . . .?'

I do not drink tea or coffee, so I firmly said, 'No.'

After some time, he hesitantly asked, 'Milk?'

I do not usually take milk either but I didn't want to hurt his feelings by denying everything he offered. So I nodded my head in affirmation.

He went to the other side of the partition and talked to his wife in Oriya. 'Madam has come all the way from a big city. She is helping our village by establishing a school so that our children can study well. This rain may not stop for some time. Please give her a glass of milk because she is our guest.'

I know Sanskrit fairly well since I learnt it at home. As a result, I can understand many Indian languages. I may not be able to speak it fluently but I can certainly understand Oriya to a great extent. My host thought that I did not understand Oriya because I had taken a translator with me. So he felt free to talk about me to his wife in Oriya.

Hearing her husband's words, the wife was very upset. 'The baby is crying continuously. I feel as if the pouring rain and this crying baby are having a jugalbandi!' she said in an irritated tone. 'The lady sitting outside has grey hair but no common sense. We are poor people. We also have to take care of a child. I have only one glass of goat's milk left for the baby. In this village, I have to work hard even to get this milk. If madam wants tea, I can give her a few teaspoons of milk. If she wants to eat fish, I can fetch them from the pond and prepare an excellent fish curry. If she wants to eat *pakhala* [leftover rice and water, an ordinary people's delicacy], it is already there. But she shouldn't ask for an expensive drink such as milk.'

My host requested his wife, 'Please don't be so rude. It doesn't suit you. You are a kind-hearted woman. Fortunately, madam can't understand Oriya. Because of this rain, she has come to our hut. Otherwise, she would have left for Bhubaneswar. She is yet to finish her work for the day. Her translator told me that she is a vegetarian and can't eat fish. She may not be used to eating pakhala either. Unfortunately, she does not drink tea. Offering just water isn't enough. What else can we give her? We only have milk. Is it not true that we should look after our guest well? You can take half of the milk, add water and boil it. Madam can share the milk with the baby.'

Silence fell in the hut. I was shocked hearing the conversation on the other side of the partition.

After some time, the owner brought milk for me in a small tumbler. This was the first time I realized that when a guest demands something, however small it might seem, it might be hard for the host to provide it, especially in a poor country like ours. If the guest has expensive habits, it will definitely hurt the host. In my ignorance and on his insistence, I had agreed to drink milk. But I was not even aware that I was snatching the share of a little baby. I felt ashamed. It was not possible for me to eat fish or drink tea. What should I do?

A few minutes later, my translator returned from the shop chewing the Pan Parag he had gone looking for. I told him, 'Tell my host that I am on fast today as I fast on all Wednesdays. I had forgotten that today is a Wednesday. I don't take anything other than water. So tell him no milk, please.'

My translator was baffled, because he had seen me having milk in the morning for breakfast. But he conveyed to the host what I had told him anyway.

My host asked, 'Nobody fasts on Wednesdays. Usually, people fast on Mondays, Thursdays, Fridays or Saturdays. Why are you fasting today?'

I said, 'I fast on Wednesdays for Buddha.'

Our host felt very sorry that I did not eat or drink anything in his hut but he was happy that he had done his best.

From that day onward, I gave up drinking milk.

5

Changing India

It was 25 April 1979—the first time I went to the USA. My destination was Boston. It was the beginning of summer when I landed at Logan airport. The days were long now so there was still light outside though it was late in the day. I saw that there was still some snow left on the ground—the last vestiges of a long winter.

I was last in the immigration queue. I had had a stopover in Paris and the waiting period for the connecting flight had been long because India was not a frequently travelled to country. So I was tired after the thirty-hour journey.

When my turn came, the stern-faced immigration officer asked me for my passport and started questioning me. 'Lady, why have you come to the United States?'

I handed my passport over to the officer and said, 'My husband is working for Data General Computer

Company and his duration of stay here is eight months. He has already been in Boston for a month and I want to join him. That's why I have come here.'

'How long do you want to stay?'

'A maximum of six months.'

'Are you working in India? If yes, show me your leave certificate and salary slip.'

Expecting these questions, I had brought those certificates with me and I showed them to him.

'How long will you stay in Boston?'

'I will be here for a few months. My brother is in Berkeley and I want to visit him after that.'

'Show me your return ticket and how much money you have brought from your country.'

'I have five hundred dollars.' I showed him the ticket and the money.

He looked at me with disbelief, stamped my visa for three months and gave my passport back to me. Then, he looked at me and said, 'What is that? What are you wearing?'

'I am wearing an Indian traditional sari. It is our national dress.'

'Hmm, you are from India. Where is this country? Is it near Japan? Or in Africa?'

'No, it is a part of Asia.'

'How do you know English?'

'In India, we have many languages. Along with our national language, we also learn English at school.'

His shift was about to end and another officer joined him and asked me, 'What are you wearing on your forehead?'

'This is known as bindi or kumkum. Most Indian women wear it.'

'Is that a caste mark?' he said.

His friend said, 'Oh, I remember learning about India in a documentary. It said that people in your country burn widows. Also, there are only two classes of people there, maharajas and beggars. You play with snakes, and cows are allowed to wander on the highways. Is that true?'

I was taken aback by his rude remarks. 'Burning widows was stopped several hundred years ago. It is not true that every widow in every state was burnt anyway. There are no maharajas left in India. It is a democratic country. In India, you see snakes only in the zoos or in the forests, just like in any other Asian country. Also, cows wander in villages on the road but not on the highways,' I explained patiently.

'Do you own an elephant?'

I laughed and said, 'It is not easy to own an elephant, but I have seen many.'

'That's enough. You can go now.'

I thanked them and went to the customs counter. In those days, customs was very tough on visitors. A customs officer asked me, 'What did you bring from India?'

'Oh, there are very few Indian stores here and we don't have a car. Hence, I have brought some masalas from home.'

The customs officer treated me like I was carrying diseases instead of masalas. He used a stick and asked me to point out and identify the masalas.

When I came out of there, I felt very dejected.

I have always been proud of my country because of our history and five thousand years of civilization. Even today, we continue the practices of the Indus Valley Civilization but other contemporary civilizations of that time have disappeared from the face of the earth. Our contribution to science in the olden days was outstanding and we were very good in astrophysics. We created music and dance forms and wrote books on them. We also generated enormous volumes of literature in the form of poetry, prose and dramas. Our civilization has stored two-thousand-year-old inscriptions that indicate that we knew writing. Our monumental temples show the zenith of architecture but for an outsider we are nothing but a poverty-stricken land of snake charmers and elephants, maharajas and beggars. It was not a good feeling.

Years rolled on. Infosys was formed along with many other companies in Bangalore. In time, Bangalore became the hub of the Indian software industry. The word 'Bangalored' itself became synonymous with outsourcing.

Today, Bangalore International Airport has many flights connecting directly to the USA and the rest of the world. Going abroad is as easy as taking a domestic flight. The next generation has become very confident, well-travelled, tech-savvy and hardworking. The West has finally woken up and taken note of this change.

In 2009, I went to Bogota, the capital of Columbia, in South America. I was visiting Columbia to deliver a talk on 'Lessons in Life'. My experiences at the Infosys Foundation had become very popular and valuable and people wanted to know all about them. I finished my talk and flew from Bogota to Miami, USA.

As always, I was last in the immigration queue. When my turn came, the visa officer was a young, lively African American. He saw me and knew that I was last, so he was quite relaxed and started asking me questions. I was ready to answer the monotonous questions. But this time it was different.

He asked, 'Oh, lady, you are from India?'

As a woman, I talk a lot. As a teacher, I talk a lot. As a trustee, I talk a lot. As an analyst, I talk a lot. I usually talk four times more than the average person. But sometimes, I talk less and listen more.

'Yes, I am from India,' was all I said.

'I know your national dress, the sari. It is really pretty. I like the way you wear it.'

I smiled and said, 'Thank you.' I did not have any other reply.

'Where are you coming from?'

Hesitantly, I said, 'I am coming from a city called Bangalore from the south of India.'

'Oh, I know Bangalore. It is a software hub. Lots of people from Bangalore come to Miami for a holiday. Lady, how long do you want to stay in our country?'

I was flying from Miami to San Francisco and then from San Francisco back to India.

I replied, 'Three days.'

'Why only three days?'

'I have work with Stanford University and after that I will go back home.'

'No, no. You should know that our country has great universities and beautiful states. You can't finish seeing our country in just three days.'

He stamped a six-month visa on my passport and said, 'Can I ask you some questions? Anyway, you have a visa now.'

I nodded my head.

'How is it that you Indians are so good? You are no-nonsense people. Your name is never on the terrorist list. Most of you are very professional.'

I smiled proudly and said, 'We are trained to be that way.' Now, I started asking him questions. 'How do you know so much about India?'

'Oh, it is not difficult. There are lots of Indian restaurants in Miami. On the weekends, I go there and eat.'

'What do you like there?'

'Good Indian food—tandoori chicken, chicken tikka, kebab and biryani.' He finished his work and got up.

I collected my bags and he joined me as I walked to customs. 'You know, lady, I like Bollywood songs,' he said. 'There are also Bollywood dance classes in Miami. By the way, I really like Kajol. She is very talented.'

By then, we had reached customs. 'It was really nice to meet you, lady. Have a good stay.'

As he walked away, I heard him humming '*Suraj hua madhham, chand dhalne laga*' from the movie *Kabhi Khushi Kabhie Gham* in an American accent.

As I walked on, the customs officer did not even look at me. He just waved at me.

I found myself outside the airport with the passport in my hands. I was wondering what had changed in the last thirty years. It is not software alone. It is India in the eyes of the West. India is no longer a poverty-stricken land of snake charmers and elephants. The immigrant Indians in other countries, confident Indians at home who have created wealth, our next generation that has worked hard and competed successfully with the West and our children who are now global citizens have changed India's image in even a small airport like Miami.

I smiled as I looked at my Indian passport.

6

Genes

Anant was an unskilled worker in his early twenties who came to our house one day looking for work. When my grandfather opened the door, Anant requested him, 'Please let me work in your house. Just give me two meals a day. I have no money or family in this world and nowhere to go.'

My grandfather took pity on him and said, 'Boy, you can stay in our house as long as you want. But after some time, you should get married and take care of your family. For that, you will need money. Without skills, one can't earn money. I will teach you to perform pujas and I will pay you a hundred rupees per month as long as you stay with us.'

Anant was taken aback. He never expected to be paid to learn and even get free accommodation. In those days, a hundred rupees was a large sum of money. Anant became the man Friday of our house. All my childhood memories are inevitably linked with Anant.

As man Friday, Anant would perform all tasks without question. My grandmother would call out to him, 'Anant, go and bring vegetables from the market.' My uncle would tell him, 'Anant, go to the post office and get me some postcards. On the way back, get me a newspaper from the bazaar.' My aunt would say, 'Anant, will you pluck flowers from the garden for me? I have to make a garland for God!' I always went with Anant and accompanied him on his errands. Anant never complained and always smiled while he worked. He used to sit with my grandfather every day and learned to perform puja with devotion.

One day, my grandmother lost her gold bangle. It was a wedding gift from her father. Hence, there was a lot of sentimental attachment to it; she started sobbing. Everybody at home scanned the entire house but we did not find it. When night fell, my crying grandmother lit a lamp and told Anant to place it in front of the tulsi plant. When he went there, he saw a shining piece of metal in the mud. When he picked it up, he realized that it was my grandmother's gold bangle and ran back to give it back to her. My grandmother was extremely happy with him. She realized that she must have dropped the bangle while she was watering the plant. Grandfather gave Anant a hundred rupees as a reward and declared, 'Your honesty makes you a role model for all the people in our house.' However, Anant refused to accept the money. He said, 'A reward is for someone who is not family. I consider myself a part of this family. I will not take your money.'

On another occasion, Anant wanted to buy something for himself but he had run out of money. So he took an advance of fifty rupees from my grandfather against his next monthly allowance. At the beginning of next month, my grandfather gave Anant a hundred rupees, forgetting to deduct the advance. Anant immediately said, 'Ajja, please keep fifty rupees with you because you have already given it to me as an advance.' My grandfather was proud of Anant for his honesty and patted his back.

My grandfather told the whole family about this incident and said, 'If Anant had kept the hundred rupees, I wouldn't have known and he would have made a profit of fifty rupees. Even though Anant is in need of money, his honesty and integrity are more important to him. So he will never take money that does not belong to him.'

After a few years, Anant got married to a girl from another village. Her father was the chief priest in their village. Since Anant knew how to perform pujas very well, he decided to move to his wife's village and help her father take care of the local temple. We all cried the day Anant left home and we felt like a beloved daughter was leaving after marriage. Long after he was gone, my grandfather always remembered him and we often talked about him.

All of us children grew up and settled in the city. Time passed by, things changed and Anant faded into the background as a fond memory. Neither our grandparents nor our ancestral house in the village remained.

Several years passed. One day, I was pleasantly surprised to see an unusual visitor in my office. It was Anant. I remembered the time we had spent together wandering in the village and learning many things. Those days were filled with simple and unforgettable moments. I went and touched his feet as a mark of respect. He looked embarrassed. I told him to sit down and made him comfortable. He had brought a young man with him.

Slowly, Anant started talking. 'How is your uncle? Where is your brother? I haven't met you for a long time. Things have changed so much.' He inquired about every member of my family and I replied with all the details.

Finally, Anant introduced the young man sitting next to him, 'This is Hari, my grandson. I have one daughter. He is her son. Hari studied in our village. Then, he went to study in the neighbouring town and has just finished college. He appeared for . . .'

Anant turned to his grandson and asked him, 'What exam have you given? I have forgotten the name.'

Confidently and proudly, Hari said, 'IIT entrance.'

Anant continued, 'He has got admission in Chennai. He has taken a bank loan to pay his college fees because my son-in-law cannot afford the expenses for his education. Hari says that IIT is a very good college in our country. I don't know. But the boy is hell-bent on going there. Can you please help him in any way?'

I replied, 'I can't help you from the Foundation because I know you personally. At the Foundation, we help only those people who don't know anyone and have nowhere else to go. But I will help you with my personal funds.' I saw a sigh of relief on Hari's face and happiness on Anant's.

I thought, 'Here is this bright, young boy who is going to IIT. I am sure that he will get a very good job later and earn lots of money. Why should I give him a scholarship? I would prefer to give him a loan.' I saw Hari's marks and was glad to find out that he had got admission in computer science.

I asked Hari, 'How much money are you short of?'

'Though I have applied for a scholarship and a bank loan, I still need fifty thousand per year to complete the course.'

'Okay, in that case, I will lend you two lakhs now and you can use it for your education. Please remember that it is not a gift. It is a loan without interest. You should return it as soon as you can afford to return it, even if it is a small amount of money per month. This way, I can lend the amount to another bright child like you and the chain can continue. Your grandfather is one of the most honest persons I have ever known. I am sure that the same culture and genes flow in the family.'

'Do I need to sign any document for this loan?' asked Hari.

'No, your word of honour is more than enough. After all, you are Anant's grandson.'

Anant said, 'Please don't worry. Hari will definitely return the money.'

I gave the loan and forgot about the incident.

Years later, I was travelling from Chennai to Bangalore. My flight was delayed and I was waiting at the airport. I saw a well-dressed young man sitting alone and waiting for the same flight. He was engrossed in reading some journals and I noticed his laptop, which was getting charged beside him. He seemed very familiar. After some time, he switched on his laptop and started working on it. When we were called to board the flight, he went to business class. I was left wondering where I had seen him.

That same evening, I went for a speaker series to a college where I was teaching. I sat in the last row because I was late. The goal of the speaker series was to inspire youngsters. I saw that the young man I had seen at the airport was one of the speakers and he spoke very well.

He said, 'I come from a small village and never had money while I was growing up. But I studied in IIT. Today, I am a self-made man. My experience has showed me that we can make life for ourselves. You can achieve whatever you want in life with self-motivation.'

I suddenly realized that he was Anant's grandson, Hari.

I asked my colleague sitting next to me, 'Who is he and why was he invited here by our college?'

'Hari is hardly twenty-eight, but he has become rich by making money in a hedge fund. He is a financial wizard. He comes from a very humble background. So we invited him to be a role model for our students.'

Hari continued his speech and I listened with rapt attention. Then I got an emergency call from my office and I left in the middle of his question and answer session.

I decided to get in touch with him and found his number easily on the Internet. I called Hari the next day. Hari's personal assistant picked up the phone and said, 'What can I do for you?'

I told her my name and said that I wanted to talk to Hari. She consulted Hari and then told me, 'Sir is very busy.'

'Please tell him that I want to talk to him for a minute.'

Hari came on the line. He was courteous and made inquiries about how I was doing. Finally, I asked him, 'How is Anant?'

He said, 'My grandfather passed away a few years ago.' I felt sad and did not know what to say but he ended the conversation and said, 'I'm sorry, I have to go. Thank you for calling.'

I felt the loss of an old friend. But something else was also nagging at me.

I thought, 'Hari never even talked about returning the loan. That money may be a small amount for me, but I know from my experience that he will never return the money. People who intend to return a loan don't end their conversations like this.'

I was very upset that Hari had cheated me. When someone gets cheated, that person gets upset not because they have lost money but because he or she realizes that they have been foolish enough to be tricked by someone. That hurts one's ego and I am no exception. I always thought that I understood people better and could forecast the results of various situations because I have been in the public field for a long time. When I am fooled, I realize that I am still a student.

Soon, I cooled down. I knew that anybody else in my position would have done the same thing. Anant was a man of integrity, so I had trusted both Anant and Hari.

As a teacher, a mother and a woman, I am used to giving sermons without being asked. I picked up the phone and called Hari to give him a piece of my mind. Fortunately, he picked up the phone himself.

I calmly said, 'Hari, I wanted to give you a gentle reminder. I know that Anant would have handed down his values and principles to you. So, if you remember, you have to return the loan of two lakhs.'

With an equally cool voice, Hari replied, 'My grandfather worked in your house for a meagre salary of a hundred rupees for years. He was an assistant to every member of your family. It was nothing but exploitation. In fact, you should pay our family more money. However, to honour my grandfather, I have not asked you for anything.' Then he disconnected the phone.

I realized then that only diseases and not honesty and integrity are passed down to the next generation through genes.

7

Helping the Dead

Vinayak was a college dropout in his early twenties. He came from an economically backward family. Vinayak's father was a timekeeper in a textile mill and his family lived in a chawl. His parents always wanted him to complete his degree and get a job so that he could ease their financial burden. Vinayak got a few interview calls for jobs but he was rejected because his communication skills in English was not good. After the rejections, he went for English classes but his spoken language never improved. His friends Banya, Bapu, Murali and others also lived in the same neighbourhood and had similar backgrounds.

Vinayak was the go-to man of his chawl. He babysat children, brought medicines for old people, got groceries for somebody and fetched water for the house among other things. His favourite of all the tenants was Usha

Tai's mother-in-law, Tunga Bai, who lived on the ground floor. She was old and could barely walk. She always sat outside on a charpoy in front of her *kholi* and counted her prayer beads. Whenever she saw Vinayak she would say, 'Bala, sit down for five minutes. You run around so much. You are a real *paropakari* in the chawl. Have a cup of tea. It is my share of tea, don't worry.'

Vinayak's helpful nature made him quite popular in his chawl but you need money to survive in this world. He always dreamt of becoming a peon in a government office. He applied to many places but there were many aspirants for the same job. Since he did not have any additional qualifications compared to others, he was always rejected. His contacts were also among the same level of people as him and hence the recommendations from them did not help him in getting a job either.

Vinayak always looked forward to the Ganapati festival, which is a big event in Maharashtra. A great political leader, Lokmanya Tilak, started this festival about a century ago. Good dramas and public speeches are showcased during the festival. The idol of Lord Ganapati is kept in a public place and worshipped for nine days. The decoration of the mantap depends upon the creativity of the organizers. Now there are competitions among the mantaps. Usually, there is an organizing committee consisting of men and women of the same age group. This committee plans a month ahead for the festival.

All the events require money and labour. Labour is normally free because many people volunteer but money is usually a problem. The organizers go from door to door to collect money. If the Ganapati is kept in a commercial area, the organizers collect more money. Unfortunately, Vinayak's Ganapati was not in a commercial area. Hence, his collection was moderate.

Sometimes, things happen in unexpected ways. One day, Vinayak and his friends went to a bank in the neighborhood with a receipt book and a donation box to collect money. The bank manager was very upset to see Vinayak and his friends since a lot of people came to the bank asking for donations. But this time, he was even more upset because he had a foreign client sitting in front of him.

It was Jim's first visit to India. He was writing a book about how Indian culture has survived despite foreign rule, various invasions and cultural diversity. Jim had come to the bank to encash his traveller's cheques and asked the bank manager who these kids were.

'Why are you not allowing them to meet you?' asked Jim.

The bank manager casually replied, 'Oh! Don't worry about it. It is very common to ask for donations during the Ganapati festival season.'

Jim had never seen the Ganapati festival and wanted to visit the local mantap. He asked Vinayak, 'Can I come to see and take some photographs for my book?'

Vinayak understood Jim's English and agreed immediately.

Jim came and saw the different activities that were part of the festival. He saw volunteers setting up the pandal, making the stage, decorating it with crêpe paper flowers, stitching colourful curtains and cutting thermocol sheets to make figurines. Amidst all this, the drama rehearsals were also going on in full swing.

While talking to them, he realized that none of them were related to each other and were of different castes. He was amazed to see the total integrity. When he left, he gave a hundred-dollar bill to the Ganapati fund. Vinayak's joy knew no bounds. He immediately ran to the bank and got it encashed. It came to five thousand rupees. This was a big sum from a single donor and was completely unexpected. Vinayak decided not to spend this money unless it was really needed.

Soon, the festival was over with great pomp and show. There was some money left. When the organizers counted the money the next day, it amounted to almost ten thousand rupees. It was a big sum for them. Usually, only two to three thousand would remain every year and the organizing committee would go to a local restaurant and treat themselves to dinner after all their hard work. This was a rare treat since they could not afford to go to such restaurants otherwise.

But this year the money was way too much. Banya said, 'Shall we have beer this year?'

Bapu said, 'How about we go for a picnic and enjoy ourselves?'

Lata said, 'We should buy a microphone set so that we won't need to hire one every year.'

Murali suggested, 'We can keep this money in a bank in a fixed deposit. Then we will get interest and we can use it next year.'

Banya said again, 'Let's just share it so that we can all do whatever we want.'

Vinayak was still thinking about what he had seen that morning. He was in no mood to reply. He was upset because Thunga Bai, who was so dear to him, had died and her body was lying in front of her kholi. That morning he had seen Usha Tai worrying about the cremation. Vinayak knew her precarious financial position. Apart from the sadness of the death, it was the expenses that were making her cry. Her husband, Sakharam, had a weak heart. The rent of the cremation van was too much for them to afford and Usha Tai was afraid that the stress would affect her husband's health. Since it was the end of the month, none of the people in the chawl were able to extend help since they themselves had no money left.

Vinayak took a decision. 'Let us help Usha Tai with the cremation,' he said. 'We are four boys here. We can carry the dead body to the cremation ground and save that expense for Usha Tai. Then we can think about what to do with the money that we have left.'

Everyone was shocked at Vinayak's decision. Banya quietly said, 'We are in a festive mood. Don't spoil it with such work.'

Vinayak did not listen to him. 'If you want, you can support me. Otherwise, I will ask someone else to help me,' he said.

Banya said, 'I don't have any experience carrying dead bodies to the cremation ground. How can I come?'

Vinayak replied, 'Nobody has any experience. There's always a first time.'

Vinayak's parents also raised an objection. 'Oh, my

child! How can you go to the cremation ground when both your parents are alive?'

'But Aai, it is not bad work. One should help. Sooner or later, all of us are going to die right here in this crowded chawl. If we don't help our neighbours, please remember that nobody will be there to help us either.'

His parents pondered over the wisdom in Vinayak's words. After a few moments, his mother said, 'Vinayak, you are absolutely right. You have our blessings. We are proud to have a son like you.'

His friends, however, followed him reluctantly. All of them went to the cremation ground and found that they had to pay some money there. Vinayak took the money from the kitty and paid the required amount.

Suddenly, Vinayak got an idea. He said, 'There must be many people in this city who are very poor and have nobody to help them cremate or bury their dead ones. They could be from any community. Why can't we help some of them? We can donate the remaining money towards that purpose. We won't get into the religious part of the cremation. That is left to the family. I am aware that we may be able to help only a few people, but it is better to spend towards a needy cause than to waste the money having beer. Don't you think that we should help people, particularly at such a time when they can't even think straight because their mind is preoccupied with thoughts of losing a loved one?'

Banya and Bapu did not like the idea at all but Lata was very enthusiastic. She said, 'Vinayak, that is brilliant. Everybody does philanthropy in different ways—building schools, providing clothes to the needy, giving books and donating blood—but I really liked your idea. Last year, I went to Rajkot to see my uncle and I told him that I wanted to visit a special place there. He took me to the cremation ground. I was so scared. But it was amazing and beautiful. It was painted well, had nice outer walls—'

'Why should they have walls? Nobody is going to run away from there anyway,' Banya joked.

'Banya, shut up. Let us listen to Lata. She was saying something,' said Vinayak.

Lata continued, 'It had a Shiva temple and a nice garden, shady trees and sheds with benches and water arrangements. The atmosphere soothes and consoles the grieving people to a large extent.'

'We are not rich to make all these arrangements in our city. But the least we can do is help the poorest of the poor in their last journey. If you agree, we can split the remaining amount, but I will use my share for this purpose. I haven't earned this money. It is public money and it should reach the public,' said Vinayak decisively.

Lata immediately said, 'I will give my share too!'

Everybody else looked at each other's faces and said, 'We will also join you.'

Vinayak's hidden leadership now came to the fore. He said, 'Let's make a volunteer group. We'll call ourselves Mukti Sena and we will help poor people.'

'Where will we search for poor people who need help with their dead?' asked Bapu.

'We can start with a government hospital. My friend is a ward boy in one of the hospitals. I am sure that there are many poor people suffering like Usha Tai,' said Vinayak.

Thus, the Mukti Sena's journey began. Soon, they realized that the money they collected was nothing compared to the number of people who needed their help. Some people could not afford to give any money while others gave a few hundred rupees. Now, Vinayak and his team had to think seriously about how long they would be able to continue like this.

The news reached the mill union through Vinayak's father who worked there. The mill union offered to give bundles of free cloth. Still, the Mukti Sena continued to fall short of money in their initial years. Vinayak learnt that economic status is formed like a pyramid. The poor people stay at the bottom but they are also the real users and donors for such causes. Vinayak knew that, over a period of time, they could collect sufficient money for their day-to-day operation.

As Vinayak and his team grew older, they required some money for their livelihood. But Vinayak said, 'We won't take even a rupee from Mukti Sena's fund.'

Once a volunteer becomes a paid worker, there is always a chance of corruption making its way into the organization. So they decided that Mukti Sena would be an all-volunteer organization and people would get other jobs for their livelihood. Almost all the members decided to work on their own. This would give them flexibility and time to contribute to Mukti Sena as well as obtain their own source of income. By this time, the word had spread about Mukti Sena and its honest volunteers. Many people came to help Vinayak and his team set up their individual businesses.

Today, Mukti Sena has thirty volunteers who work day and night. All of them are entrepreneurs who earn a small income to take care of their family. These entrepreneurs run grocery shops, children's nurseries, bicycle lending shops, paper distribution shops and printing shops among others. Whenever a Mukti Sena call comes, these volunteers always have a substitute to look after their shops until they come back. Their business never suffers because of their absence.

Even today, Vinayak says that when a person is dead, caste is never an issue. One's birth only decides how one's body should be disposed of. He says, '*Hindu, Muslim, Sikh, Isaai, sab ko mera salaam.*'

8

Three Ponds

In the olden days, ponds were the only source of water in villages if there were no rivers nearby. Hence, the villagers looked after their pond very well. They cleaned it every year and removed the silt. Each family sent one person to help clean the pond. Nobody was paid any money for this because the pond was an asset of the village. Every year, the villagers worshipped the water in the pond because they considered the water to be like the holy water of the Ganga.

There are different types of ponds: some are used for irrigation, some as a source of drinking water and some are used for both. If the pond was very large and the other shore could not be seen, it was called a *samudra* or ocean, hence the names Shanti Samudra and Vyasa Samudra, among others. Usually, ponds are named after the person who built them, such as kings, queens, rich merchants and powerful commanders.

In my vast experience of travelling in India, I found that every pond is sacred to its village and there is always a story behind the building of the pond. Inevitably, the stories say that Ganga travelled below the earth and appeared in the pond so that people could have water. That is why the water is referred to as holy water or *Gangajal*.

I have seen many ponds in different parts of India but the story of three separate ponds in Karnataka have left a lasting impression on me.

Ammani's Condition

It was the time of the East India Company and the British ruled our land. Ammani was an illiterate woman who lived near Kolar. She kept cows and buffaloes and her job was to deliver milk to the people living nearby. Kolar is a drought-prone area and she regularly saw people struggling to fetch water. Ammani always wanted to do something about this.

One day, she heard that a British camp was being set up near the village. The middleman who knew both English and Kannada came to the village in search of milk, curd, ghee and butter to supply to the British soldiers in the camp. When the news spread, everybody told the middleman that they wanted to sell to the camp.

But Ammani told the middleman, Ramappa, 'I will supply milk to the camp only on one condition. I don't want money.'

Ramappa was surprised. 'You mean you want to supply free to these *firangis*? These white men?'

'When did I say that? After all, I am a poor person.'

'Please make good money now because you are selling in bulk. Make hay while the sun shines. This is a government office. You are guaranteed money, unlike with private parties. If you miss this, you won't get this opportunity again. Be wise,' he advised her.

'Don't get me wrong. I want to sell. But I don't want money every month. It has to be kept with the British officers. You have also just said that they are reliable government people.'

'You mean to say that you will collect the money only at the end? I don't understand this.'

But Ammani insisted that she would provide milk to the British only on this condition. So Ramappa left and decided to talk to the British officers about this strange request.

The next day, Ramappa told officer George, 'There

is a very strange woman in this village. She wants to supply milk, curd and ghee but she does not want to collect money.'

George was curious. 'Bring that woman here. I want to talk to her.'

The next day, Ammani went to meet the officer. In those days, Indians were scared of the firangis. They were always worried that they might be punished without reason. Their colour was different, their language was different and India was a British colony. But Ammani went without fear. She did not know English but she knew what she was going to say.

When she reached the British camp and met George, she said, 'Sir, I am ready to supply whatever you ask for. However, the money should be kept with you. I will take it later.'

The concept of a bank was not there at the time so George thought that Ammani was scared of keeping the money at home. He asked, 'Are you scared of the thieves or relatives who will come and take your money because you are all alone?'

She smiled and said, 'No, sir, that is not the reason.'

'Then what is it?'

'I will tell you later. I am sure that you will respect that.'

Officer George liked Ammani and agreed to her request. Soon after, Ammani started supplying milk, curd and ghee to the camp. The quality of her products was better than other people's and she was very punctual. However, she became a laughing stock of her village because she chose not to take money from the British. Ammani continued to supply to the people living nearby in her village and managed her monthly expenses even though she was not getting any money from the British camp.

Years passed. Everyone in the camp knew Ammani for her honesty and the quality of her products. Over time, Ammani replaced many villagers who were supplying milk and other products. She became the single source of supply to the British camp. All the officers were friendly with her.

One day, officer George came to talk to Ammani. He said, 'Ammani, you should take your money. It is now a huge amount and it is not fair on my part to keep it for such a long time. We might change camps within a year. We really respect your honesty, and we should be honest with you too.'

'Thank you, sir, for informing me in advance. Along with my money, I want help from you and your soldiers.'

'Oh, you want to build a big bungalow?' the officer joked.

'No, sir, I want a pond.'

'What?' The officer was surprised. 'Are you aware that it is not easy to construct a pond in this hard stone area? It requires a lot of manpower. The money itself is not sufficient.'

'Sir, I beg you. That is precisely the reason why I didn't take the money. If I had taken it, I would have spent it all by this time. Since I am a widow, my relatives would have forcibly taken it from me. Sir, you don't understand the difficulties of women in the hot summer. Please do this for me.'

George thought about it. It was a difficult job. He appreciated Ammani's honesty and her concern for people. So he said, 'Let me talk to my boss and see if he can ask our soldiers to do this on a volunteer basis.'

In the end, kind-hearted George and the volunteer soldiers built the pond. The pond became the source of drinking water for the entire village. People did not have to go far to fetch water any more and, today, the pond is still known as Ammani's Pond.

Today, India is independent and Ammani is no more. Still, the pond stands witness to her generous gift to the village.

A Wedding Gift

Let me now tell you the story of the Navalgund pond. Navalgund is a fairly big town in northern Karnataka. Long ago, the village chief was a man named Rame Gowda. He had two lovely daughters, Channamma and Neelamma.

Though Navalgund's land was fertile, it was heavily dependent on rain, and life in Navalgund was very difficult. There was no water or stream nearby. Several wells were dug in search of water but there was not even a drop of water in them. Men and women walked miles to get a few buckets of water. Rame Gowda's family was rich and lived in luxury. They had many servants who fetched water for them in bullock carts. So the family never realized the problem of the poor people.

One day, there was a panchayat meeting headed by Rame Gowda. The poor people came to the meeting and said, 'Sir, please make a pond in this village. We will work hard and help build the pond. We won't even ask for the labour charges.'

Rame Gowda said, 'It is not easy to build a pond. You may say that there are no labour charges. However, we still require a lot of money to build it. Let every rich man in the village contribute something towards the pond.

Then we can think about it and decide.' But no rich man was ready to give money.

In those days, every rich man had plenty of labourers and many of them were bonded labourers. So the rich people in Navalgund never cared to understand the difficulties of fetching water. Neelamma was standing behind the pillar when the conversation was going on. She knew that her father could have funded the construction of the pond because he was the richest man in the village. She also realized that other rich people were waiting for Rame Gowda to contribute some money himself. But nothing happened and the meeting was adjourned.

Neelamma felt very sad. She knew the problems of fetching water because she knew the difficulties of her maid. One day, without informing anyone, Neelamma had walked with the maid to get a bucket of water. It was a Herculean task. But Neelamma knew that her father would never listen to her. So she kept quiet.

A few years went by. Channamma and Neelamma grew up and Rame Gowda found two rich sons-in-law. The weddings were held with great pomp. When Channamma and Neelamma were about to leave their father's home, he asked them, 'Daughters, you are leaving this town. What do you want as a gift?'

Channamma said, 'I want a bullock cart filled with jewellery.'

'Sure, my daughter,' said Rame Gowda.

Neelamma did not say anything.

'Neelamma, what do you want?' her father insisted.

'I don't know whether you will be able to give me what I want,' she said.

That enraged Rame Gowda. 'What do you mean by that? I am the richest man in the village and have only two daughters. Look at your sister. When she asked me for a bullock cart of jewellery, I agreed. Why will I say no to you? Are you going to ask me for something extraordinary?'

Neelamma said, 'I will ask for something that you can definitely give me. But promise me that you will. Only then will I ask you.'

Rame Gowda thought that Neelamma might ask for more jewellery than her sister, or maybe she wanted land. So he said, 'Yes.'

'Father, I don't want a gram of gold or jewellery from your house. I don't even want silk saris. I do not intend to take an inch of your land. But I want a pond to be constructed in the middle of the village so that every poor person can fetch drinking water with ease.'

Rame Gowda was dumbstruck. First, he was very

upset with his daughter. Then he thought of the expense. He knew that he could afford it. He remembered his promise. He smiled and said, 'A promise is a promise. I will build a pond for you.'

Even today, the pond named after Neelamma stands in the middle of Navalgund town. Over a period of time, the pond has been expanded and decorated. But to this day, it is well maintained. Everyone must follow the strict rule of washing his or her feet before entering the pond. There is no way that the people of Navalgund can afford to contaminate the water. Today, Neelamma, Channamma and Rame Gowda are no more but everybody remembers Neelamma's concern for the people of Navalgund.

Bhagirathi

Now, we come to my favourite pond story. If you travel from Hangal to Haveri, you come across a sleepy village known as Kallakere (colloquially known as Kalakeri). There is a beautiful pond with clear water here. There is also a Shiva temple in front of the pond. This pond stands out because of the unusual lotuses and leaves in it. These lotuses look very welcoming. But if you go near the pond, you will feel that the lotuses are moving away from you. It is, after all, Bhagirathi's pond.

Long, long ago, Mallana Gowda was the village headman. He had seven sons and all of them were married. His youngest daughter-in-law was Bhagirathi. She was very beautiful and an extremely good-natured young woman. She was soft-spoken, an introvert who never expressed her feelings in public. Her husband was an officer in the army on active duty. So he was away a lot. Bhagirathi's in-laws looked after her. She was popular with her friends, in-laws and all the people in the village.

Mallana Gowda ordered the building of a pond in the village. A pond was constructed but there was no water in it. He was really worried. If the pond did not have water, people and farmers would continue to suffer. He had spent a lot of money to dig this pond and had performed many pujas but still there was no water.

One day, the elders in the village were discussing something in a very hush-hush manner. Bhagirathi, who was in the garden doing some work, could hear them clearly. Nobody noticed her presence.

Somebody said to Mallana Gowda, 'Sir, there is only one way you can get water in the pond. A married woman should pray for the welfare of the people wholeheartedly and ask God for water. Then, water may come. But . . .' he stopped.

'Oh, what is so tough about that? Every woman in the village can do this,' replied another man.

'But there is a condition. Once the water gushes into the pond, the person who prays may not be able to come out of the water and may eventually drown. Is anyone ready for this?'

Silence fell upon the group. There were many daughters-in-law in the village but no father or father-in-law opened his mouth.

'Is it so difficult to get Bhagirathi?' asked somebody.

Mallana Gowda was very upset. He shouted at him, 'Out of the entire village, why are you only thinking about my daughter-in-law? There are others too.'

'No, sir, I did not mean your daughter-in-law Bhagirathi. I meant Ganga.'

Ganga is also widely known as Bhagirathi. There is a very popular folk story in India. The story goes like this. Ganga was a river that flowed only in heaven. King Bhagiratha prayed for Ganga to come down to earth and help people. He made many penances and begged her. So she came at his request. That is why she is also called Bhagirathi. Even today, we can see the statue of King Bhagiratha in Gangotri, the source of the Ganga.

Bhagirathi heard the conversation and went to her room. She did not sleep that night. She thought to herself,

'My husband is selflessly serving the country in the army. What is the use of my life if I can't make a sacrifice so that everyone can live in peace and harmony?' It was a very difficult situation and her mind was in turmoil.

The next day, she told her father-in-law, 'Father, I want a small favour. I want all of us to perform a small puja at the bottom of the steps of the pond. Who knows, Bhagirathi may come.'

Her father-in-law laughed. 'My child, we have done many pujas but still we have not been able to get water. However, if it is your wish, we will do so next week.'

The next day, Bhagirathi went to her best friend's house and talked to everyone there. While departing, she had tears in her eyes. Her friend consoled her, 'Don't be so sad. Your husband will be back soon. He will be victorious. Be brave.' But Bhagirathi did not say anything.

A day later, she went to her parents' house and they were surprised to see Bhagirathi coming alone to visit them, which she had never done before. She stayed with them for two days. With tears in her eyes, she said goodbye to them. 'Bhagirathi, don't cry. Your husband will be back soon,' they said. Bhagirathi did not reply and came back to her in-laws' house.

The next day, she went and invited the entire village for the puja.

On the day of the ceremony, she dressed like a bride and her family went to perform the puja at the bottom of the pond. Once the puja was completed, everybody started going back.

Bhagirathi climbed a few steps and told her father-in-law, 'Father, I have forgotten my gold plate at the bottom of the pond. All of you please carry on. I will come and join you.' Then she climbed down and stood alone at the bottom of the pond. She folded her hands towards the sky and prayed to River Ganga. 'O Mother Ganga, please come to our village. Please fill this pond with your sweet water and make everyone prosperous. Look after the women, children, old people and animals in this village and give them water. In return, if you want to take my life, it is yours. After all, I am Bhagirathi and am named after you.'

Then she climbed the first step. Suddenly, there was thunder and wind but nobody could see anything. Water started gushing from the sides of the pond and came up to Bhagirathi's ankles. She climbed the second step. Water continued to gush in and came up to her knees. Instantly, Bhagirathi knew what was happening. She was happy and sad at the same time. She climbed the third step. Water came up to her hips. She continued to climb to the fourth step. Water came up to her armpits. She climbed the fifth step. The water reached her neck. She climbed the sixth step. Water came up to her nose. At last, she climbed the seventh step. Water passed over her head and she could not breathe any more. The thunder stopped and the winds calmed.

Mallana Gowda turned back to see what was happening. The pond continued to fill until it was full. The whole village was surprised to see the water in the pond after so many years of praying. After some time, Mallana Gowda realized that his daughter-in-law Bhagirathi was missing. He knew what had happened then. Tears started flowing from his eyes. He sat on the ground and started crying. 'O Bhagirathi my child, you were my responsibility until your husband came back. I loved you like my daughter but I never knew your plan. Is that the reason you visited your parents and friends? Is that why you dressed like a bride today and purposely forgot the gold plate? I did not know that you had heard our conversation last week. Bhagirathi, you gave your life so that others can have water. But how will I face your husband?'

Now the entire village realized that Bhagirathi had sacrificed her life for them. They were unable to enjoy the arrival of Ganga.

The next month, the war ended and Bhagirathi's husband came back victorious. He wanted to talk about his adventures and share his achievements with his wife. He purchased expensive jewellery and saris for Bhagirathi.

When he reached home, he realized that everybody was happy but also sad about something. He could not see a trace of Bhagirathi anywhere. He asked his father, 'Where is Bhagirathi? I want to meet her.'

His father did not have the courage to tell him the truth. He said, 'She has gone to her friend's house.'

Her husband left immediately for her friend's house. Even at her friend's house, the family was in tears but could not tell him the truth. Instead, they said, 'She has gone to her mother's house.'

He immediately left for her parents' house and did not get any reply from them either.

When Bhagirathi's husband was going back home, he became very thirsty. He saw there was a new pond in his village brimming with water. He got down and drank some water. It was very sweet. He looked at the pond and was unable to move. He sat there for a while.

A little boy was taking his cows to graze and stopped there for water. Bhagirathi's husband asked him, 'O my child, I have never seen this lake before. And the water is like nectar. I remember that this was empty with no water. How did this happen?' The innocent child reiterated Bhagirathi's entire story and went away.

Her husband was unable to bear the shock of losing her. He cried for Bhagirathi's sacrifice. He knew that it would be very hard to live without her and told the pond, 'My dear, wherever you are, I will be with you. I don't care whether it is a pond or a house.' And he jumped into the pond.

Even today, when you see this pond, it has unusually large-sized lotuses and leaves. When I visited the village, the lotuses enchanted me. Now there are many borewells in the village, so people do not use the pond for drinking water but it is still used as a washing pond.

I asked a fisherman there to fetch me a lotus flower from the pond. He laughed at my ignorance. He said, 'Madam, you must be an outsider. Don't you know that Bhagirathi and her husband are inside? I have never seen anybody enter this pond and pluck a flower. The flowers appear in couples but the moment you go near them, they drift away from you. The depth of the pond is so deceptive that if you try to pursue the flowers, you might even drown.'

I never knew that such blooming and beautiful flowers would have such a bittersweet story behind them.

9

No Man's Garden

As a child, I went on an excursion to a well-known temple called Someshwara. This temple is located in Lakshmeshwara town. The Someshwara temple is huge and has many beautiful sculptures and pillars. But they did not fascinate me. Instead, there was a particular stone in the courtyard of the temple that touched my heart. The stone is more than a thousand years old and has an inscription and a picture. The picture depicts many cows and buffaloes drinking water from a tank and the water that fills the tank is drawn manually from a well. This is known as 'Dharma Yetha' in Kannada. A philanthropist donates a well, builds a tank, and makes provisions to draw the water. Poor people can at least help draw water from the well and store it in the tank, which can be used by both human beings and animals. Nobody has ownership over the tank or the water. This concept has been etched in my mind ever since I was a child. Normally, when people lend a helping hand, there is always an expectation of getting something in return. But if you are a true philanthropist, the expectation decreases over time. A sense of ownership becomes meaningless in the larger context of life. This selfless helpfulness brings true happiness to a person.

Parappa was an old man in a village. His vision was good, he could hear fairly well, but walking was really hard for him. When he was younger, he could easily walk twenty miles a day. He inherited only five acres of land from his parents but, due to his hard work, he was successful in expanding it to fifty acres of land.

His son Bhimappa told him, 'Father, you have worked very hard in your time. Now the farming methodology has changed. I prefer to use the latest tractors and agricultural machinery. We don't have to come every day to inspect the labourers. Even the numbers of labourers that we need has reduced. If I require your guidance, I will definitely take your advice. You should relax and look after the house.'

So Parappa retired and his son Bhimappa took charge of the land.

Parappa had built a big house that faced the mud boundary of the village tank. This boundary is called *baduvu* in Kannada. In the village, Parappa became known as Baduvina Parappa and the baduvu became his identity. Every evening, Parappa sat in the veranda of the house and his friends joined him to discuss the village news.

Parappa was a prosperous farmer and had many servants. Bhimappa's wife had a maid called Paravva. She came and cleaned the house every day. She was very talkative and brought all the juicy news of the village. It became a regular practice for Parappa to finish his breakfast and sit in the veranda facing the baduvu and talk to Paravva while she worked. Paravva was even better than the local newspaper and gave Parappa the inside stories of the village.

Paravva also told Parappa about her domestic problems. She had a large family—her husband, his parents, two children and a brother-in-law with his three children. Her husband worked in Parappa's farm. But still, life was not easy for them.

One morning, Paravva started her news bulletin. 'There is a new disease in our vegetables. So the price of vegetables in the village has become ten times its usual price. Even the rich people are finding the vegetables expensive and are thinking twice before spending money on vegetables. One kilo of tomatoes is more expensive than two litres of milk. Oh, yesterday I had such a tough time,' she said, sighing.

'What happened?' Parappa asked.

'Yesterday, my sister and her family of five suddenly came to our house. Since they were our guests, I had to give them good food. I made roti, rice and dal but I could not get any vegetables. It was very embarrassing for me.'

'Why didn't you have vegetables?'

'How can I buy vegetables at this price? You know that our village fair is only once a week. Even though I buy vegetables at the fair, I don't have a refrigerator to store them. It is hard to get vegetables in our village any time we want.'

'Didn't you store at least a few pumpkins?' asked Parappa. It was a practice in the village to keep spare pumpkins at home because they did not get spoiled easily and did not need refrigeration.

'I had two pumpkins but I used them a few weeks ago when we had unexpected guests. I wish I had a tiny garden to grow a pumpkin plant to avoid such awkward situations. But I don't have a square inch of land near our hut.' Paravva continued, 'There are many poor people like me in our village. They can't afford to buy or grow vegetables. Vegetables are essential. It is sad that all our political parties promise us rice but not vegetables.' Then she said to herself, 'Today, there is a panchayat meeting in your house. I should keep the hall clean, dust well and prepare some snacks for the meeting.' And she went inside the house to start cleaning the hall.

Parappa started thinking about what she had said. He had never suffered from a lack of vegetables in his diet. Since he was a rich farmer, he always had land to grow some vegetables in his fields. The vegetables were sufficient for his house and he had never needed to buy them. When vegetables were in excess, he distributed them among his workers. But he could not do that all the time. His mother used to say, 'Never keep more flowers, fruits or vegetables than you need because they get spoiled very quickly and should not be wasted. They should be shared with everybody.' His mother's rule was not valid for rice, ragi and jowar grain because they did not get spoiled for months and could be stored easily.

While Parappa was pondering about Paravva's predicament, his dog Bandu started barking. Distracted, Parappa watched Bandu run after another dog. Both the dogs went near the baduvu portion of the tank. There was a lot of congress grass, ordinary grass, cactus and other unknown shrubs there. The two dogs fought and urinated there. They also slept on the grass and relaxed there in the morning sun. Suddenly, a mother pig came along with her piglets. The two dogs barked and chased her away. This was not a new sight. Parappa was used to seeing the same scene every day since the baduvu was no-man's-land and belonged to the village gram panchayat. Nobody ever bothered to clean it. It was the abode of rats, pigs, dogs and other animals.

Parappa got an idea. 'Why can't I use this land to grow vegetables for the poor people?' he asked himself. But the land itself was not flat. It was on a slope. Today, there was a gram panchayat meeting in his house and he decided to submit his proposal there.

Parappa was well respected in the village and everybody called him Ajja. Usually, Parappa did not attend any panchayat meetings since his son Bhimappa was already a member of the panchayat. So Bhimappa was surprised to see him at the meeting. All the members greeted Parappa warmly and started the meeting.

When the meeting was about to come to an end, Parappa stood up and said, 'I have an idea. Many people in our village can't afford vegetables because the prices are very high. It is difficult for them to even store a few pumpkins. The baduvu facing my house is a wasteland. Only unwanted shrubs grow there. If the panchayat allows me, I would like to clean that land, grow some vegetables and distribute it to the poor people of our village.'

Everybody was surprised at his unusual proposal.

'Ajja, I really appreciate your enthusiasm and idea,' said a young member, Suresh. 'But the panchayat office will not pay for the cleaning. It is a waste of money. The dogs and pigs won't let you grow anything there. Who will guard the garden? Who will water it? Have you thought about the details?'

Parappa replied, 'I have thought about it. I don't want the entire baduvu. I am an old man. I can only look after a portion of the land. I will spend my own money to clean it. The panchayat does not need to spend any money on this project. But I want your permission.'

'Whom will you give the vegetables to? Maybe you want to give them to your own servants. But that will be unfair because the slope is not yours,' said Suresh.

'I promise you that none of my servants will get vegetables from this garden. When the vegetables are grown, I will bring the entire harvest to the panchayat office and you can decide on the distribution. Is that acceptable?'

The panchayat members felt that this was not a practical idea but they had a lot of respect for old Parappa. So they agreed to give him a chance.

When the meeting was over, Bhimappa was very upset. 'Why do you want to get into these things at this age?' he told his father. 'Can't you enjoy your old age and relax by going to a temple, watching TV or playing with the kids? If you are unsuccessful, people will make fun of you. If you are successful, we won't benefit anyway. So, no matter what, we will run into losses. In fact, we have to spend money to clean and guard the baduvu and grow the vegetables.'

'Son, think of those people who don't have a square inch of land to call their own. Is it not our duty to help the people who are on the other side of the poverty line? These poor people don't even have a refrigerator and they buy their vegetables only once a week at the fair. I really want to help them. I don't have many expenses. Let me spend some money on this and do some good. Let people say whatever they want about me. It does not matter,' said Parappa.

'I don't know how you will manage. But please don't expect me to help you with this,' said Bhimappa harshly.

This is how Parappa's new project started. He took help of the coolies to identify how much land he needed to grow vegetables. He marked the areas and asked the coolies to clean it. It was full of plastic bags and bottles.

Then he cordoned off the area with thin bamboo woven mats, which served as a barrier that prevented animals from entering. Finally, he sowed pumpkin seeds, cucumber and green vegetables. He knew that water would not be a problem because there was a water tank on the other side of the baduvu and water flowed directly to the garden. He also made a bench near the garden and met people there. People started calling it 'Parappa's garden'.

When the plants grew and flowered, small pumpkins appeared. Parappa was so excited that people thought he was welcoming a new grandchild. When the green vegetables grew and the leaves started appearing in abundance, Parappa felt proud of his plants. But he faced many difficulties. Once, an angry pig almost shattered the bamboo wall. A few weeks later, rats took away a few cucumbers. Some mischievous children even stole a few pumpkins. So Parappa brought a watchdog to protect the garden at night. The farming season ended and a reasonable amount of vegetables had now grown.

One day, his daughter-in-law wanted some cucumbers. Parappa refused to give her any cucumbers even though she offered him money. He said, 'I can't go back on my words to the panchayat.' Paravva, his favourite maid, also made many requests, but he did not give vegetables to her either.

Eventually, he collected all the vegetables that had grown and took them to the panchayat office. He said, 'You can distribute these to anyone you like. But my humble request is that poor people should get the vegetables.'

Parappa went away without even waiting for an answer. The panchayat members were amazed at Parappa's detachment and saluted his spirit. Bhimappa realized what his father had accomplished and he was very proud of him.

Today, Parappa grows vegetables the year round in his garden by the baduvu and continues to give them to the panchayat when they are ready.

Our Parappa's garden of this century is no less than the *Dharma Yetha* of centuries past.

10

Sticky Bottoms

A few years ago, I was going out of town and was about to board a train. From a distance, I saw Venkat on the railway platform. I can never miss Venkat anywhere because he stands out in a crowd. He is tall, thin and always wears white.

The moment I saw him, I immediately got into a train compartment so that he could not see me. I went to my air-conditioned coupé where there were four seats. Three of them were already occupied. I sat on the fourth seat by the window and thought that I should start reading. As I opened my bag to get out the book, I heard, 'Oh, it is you. It is my good luck that you are on this train. I am also travelling by the same train.'

Without lifting my head, I knew that it was Venkat's voice. He was standing in front of me like a coconut tree.

'Yes, yes,' I stammered. As usual, he did not care about what I was saying.

'I thought I saw you on the platform standing next to this train. And then you disappeared so I wasn't sure. I decided to search for you. Your quick disappearance told me that you must be on this train. I was wondering how to start looking for you but, fortunately, I found you in the first compartment I searched. Ha, ha, ha,' he laughed to himself, 'my search is better than your computer search.'

Then he looked around the compartment and said, 'Oh, all the other seats are taken.' He requested the passenger sitting next to me, 'Sir, we are really good friends but we haven't seen each other for a long time. Would you mind exchanging my seat with yours?'

The occupant of the seat was a young man in his mid-twenties with earphones plugged in. He could not hear Venkat properly but understood what was happening and said, 'What is your seat number?' I was praying that he would refuse to move seats but to my misfortune he said yes. Now Venkat became my travelling companion for the next eight hours.

I have known Venkat for more than half a century. He is good-natured and helps everyone in need. But the quirk about Venkat is that he talks too much and does not even realize or care whether the other person is listening to him.

The train left the station and Venkat immediately started chatting about something inconsequential. My mind slipped away and I started recollecting incidents with Venkat over the years.

In school, Venkat was in the debate club. If the time limit for a debate was three minutes, his introduction to the subject itself was at least four minutes. All of us in the class were tired of his incessant talk. Even the teachers regularly told him to be aware and try to talk less but he would say, 'Sir, I have verbal diarrhoea and I can't help myself.' In the end, our class became more patient but Venkat did not change.

Once there was a debate competition in our school. Venkat started his speech. Knowing his nature, our teacher rang the calling bell in two minutes even though the time limit was three minutes. But Venkat continued speaking. The second bell rang warning him that he must stop. He took the calling bell from the teacher's desk, kept it in his pocket and continued talking. After a minute, our department peon came and took away his mike. Then Venkat had to step down. He never ever won a prize for debates.

Nobody in class wanted him as a teammate in any

activity because he talked continuously and gave people a headache. It also took very long to get any work done with him in the team. We all thought that he would end up being the company chairman of either Aspirin or Zandu Balm. He would make an excellent salesperson for these companies.

After we graduated from school, Venkat did not work much because he inherited money and invested it wisely. As a result, he got regular income from his investments.

Soon, our school classmates started getting married one by one and we all wondered who would get married to Venkat. We even had a bet that his wife would run away within a year of marriage—unless, of course, she was deaf. Eventually, Venkat got married to Lata. She was nice, friendly and very quiet.

After a year of marriage, I asked her, 'Lata, how do you handle Venkat's constant chatter?'

She said, 'It is very easy. I pretend that I am listening to a radio.'

'But even a radio can be turned off.'

'Well, I mentally switch off. That's all. Otherwise, Venkat is a fantastic husband. He is very kind to my family and me. He takes care of everything at home. Some people just talk a lot.' She spoke lightly and gently about her husband.

Venkat was very fond of parties and celebrations. When he had his first baby, he called us for a party. I went at the specified time but all his other friends came an hour late because they knew that the later they came the less they would have to hear Venkat's chatter. Unfortunately, I was not as smart. The moment I reached, Venkat started describing Lata's labour pains, the delivery, the baby's vaccinations and its progress through every month until the day of the party. I felt like leaving my gift on his table and running away. I had finally learnt my lesson about spending time with Venkat.

I remembered another incident. One day, Venkat came to my house just to talk. It was hard for me to say no because he is a very kind person. I told him, 'I am in a hurry. Is there anything specific you would like to discuss?'

'Not really,' he replied. 'If you are in a hurry, you go. I will wait here for you.' People at home were terrified because nobody could sit and talk to Venkat for so long.

I told him, 'Okay, in that case, I will talk to you for fifteen minutes and then I have to go.'

Venkat said, 'Sounds fine. I wanted to let you know that I am building a new house.' I knew that he would not stop for the next fifteen minutes. He continued, 'You have already seen the huge house built by my grandfather. He used so much cement that one could have easily built four houses out of it. The kitchen was so huge that it could accommodate a hundred people. We could even perform a small wedding there. The entire site was used to build the three-storey house. You know that my father is the only son of his parents. So he inherited the house and made some foolish changes listening to his expert *vaastu* friend. He removed the door from where people used to enter and shifted it to the side instead. So the side window had to be closed. He changed the beautiful red oxide floor to tiles. He even converted the first floor into an open space for religious discourses. The people who came for these discourses were all quite old. They couldn't even climb to the first floor. So he had to make a lift for them. Then he broke open the bedroom. He spent so much money in renovation that he could have built a new house instead. My mother was very upset about the changes to the ancestral home. So she started pestering me to build a new house on the same site. My wife Lata was very happy living on the second floor of the old house because it is in a very convenient location. It has good schools and shops nearby and is in a good neighbourhood. There is a park in front of our house, which is almost like a private park but it is maintained by Bangalore Corporation. I really feel that it is just like having my own personal park . . .'

I wanted to stop his rambling so I interrupted, 'Tell me, how are you building this new house?'

'Oh, I have to satisfy everyone and keep them happy. In our house, we have five people but fifty opinions. Now my son also participates in the discussions. We are demolishing the old house and building a new one in the same place. I have brought the plan just to show you. Bangalore Corporation may approve of my plan but people at home may not. So, first, I got it approved at home and now I am on my way to the corporation.'

Then he opened his plan. I saw some drawings but I was not really interested. I thought that this was a good opportunity to tell Venkat to leave. 'I think you should rush to the corporation,' I said. 'Their department will close.'

'Oh, don't worry about it. I have an agent. I told him to call me whenever the officer comes. Now it is lunch hour there. So the officer may not come back for some time.'

I was really scared that Venkat might stay for another two hours at my house. With every passing minute, I was getting fed up. But Venkat never realized it. He continued, 'See this plan. Here is the entrance to the house. The first room is a small veranda but not as small as normal verandas. It should be enough to leave the chappals outside. I want to put a few wooden benches so that people can sit down comfortably and remove or wear their slippers. Then we have another veranda where we can greet people formally. So I will keep some sofas and chairs there. You know, everyone enters the living room in our current home. Lata doesn't like that at all and I must obey her instructions because she spends most of her time at home . . .'

Just then, his cellphone rang. He picked it up and said, 'Okay.' I breathed a sigh of relief. Maybe the corporation officer was back. But he finished talking in a few seconds. Then he looked at me and said, 'Well, the corporation engineer is on vacation today. We have plenty of time now. I can explain each room to you.'

'You don't have to, Venkat. These days, you get three-dimensional pictures on the computer that you can walk through.'

'Oh, yes. You are right. I have my laptop also. I can show you.' He opened his laptop. Now I knew that I was his prisoner. I remembered the advertisement: *Fevicol ka jod hai, tootega nahin.*

I decided to be brave and end it. I got up and told Venkat, 'Sorry, Venkat. I have to go somewhere.'

He smiled at me and said, 'Your driver went for lunch a few minutes ago. I saw him leave through the window. You have to wait for him anyway. Until he comes back, I can ask for your suggestions.' Then he asked me, 'Now, where was I?'

'You've been here in front of me forever,' I said sarcastically.

As usual, Venkat did not understand. 'Oh, I thought I was in the veranda of my house,' he continued opening his laptop.

With my new-found bravado, I thought of another way of cutting him off. I got up and walked towards the main door. 'Venkat, let us do this. I will come to your house soon. Lata will also be there. We can sit down and discuss in detail then.' I stepped outside hoping to see my driver.

Now Venkat had to get up and leave.

I was brought back to the present with the sound of the *chaiwala*. I was on the train. Venkat was still chatting away. Remembering these incidents, I did not know if I could listen to him politely for the rest of the journey. The only escape route I had was to use the train toilet. But even I could not sit there for more than five minutes with the level of hygiene they have in there.

Venkat changed the subject and started telling me

about his recent trip to Japan. Now I got ready to hear about Japan—its GDP, its people, and Venkat's journey from the day he went till the day he came back. Venkat continued, 'Japanese people are extremely sensitive. They will never say what's on their minds. They show calmness outside but they are not like that inside. They feel very shy to refuse and consider it bad manners.'

Suddenly, I remembered, 'Hey Venkat, have you heard about sticky bottoms?'

Venkat did not know what it was so he stopped to think for a minute. I told him, 'In Japan, if somebody has a guest and they don't leave for a long time, the host brings a broom and keeps it upside down. They do this when they have a lot of work to do and don't have time to entertain the guest any more. The moment the guest sees the broom upside down, he or she understands. So the guest leaves politely. That person is called a Sticky Bottom.'

'Oh, that is a nice concept. Maybe I should tell Lata. When some people come and never leave our house, she can keep the broom that way.'

'Venkat, nobody in our country will understand because most of us are not that sensitive.'

I was thinking about how I could tell Venkat that he was one of them. By this time, my station had come and

I was very happy. I thought to myself, 'Why is Venkat like this? He is so insensitive and talks too much. Is it because he has a lot of energy and no hobbies, no special responsibilities and no aim in life? Or maybe it is because of anxiety. I do not know. He speaks all the time and spends all his energy.'

As I was getting ready to get down, Venkat suddenly exclaimed, 'Hey, what about my stop? Where is it?'

Then he realized that he had already passed his station.

11

Too Many Questions

At the Foundation, we buy notebooks from a factory in a village located away from Bangalore. Then, we distribute them to needy children annually.

When I went to see this factory, I found that it was in a very congested area. There were two hundred people working in shifts and all of them were poor. I decided to give these men and women a gift because Diwali was approaching.

I called the factory manager and asked him to give me the names of his two hundred employees. He was anxious to know why and when I told him that I wanted to give them gifts for Diwali, I thought that he would be really happy. Instead, he thought for a minute and said quietly, 'I will let you know tomorrow.'

The next day, the manager called me and said, 'Madam, what is the real motive behind this gesture?

Should I reduce their salary by the amount you will spend on the gift?'

'This has nothing to do with their salary,' I said.

'I hope you are not asking for a reduction or a price cut in the notebooks.'

'No, I haven't even thought about it.'

'Did any of my employees suggest that you should give them a gift?'

'No, I haven't met anyone except you from the factory.'

Somehow, he was not convinced that I wanted to give his employees gifts without a valid reason.

He continued with his questions, 'Are you going to give them gifts every year? In that case, please send me a letter stating for how many years you plan to continue giving gifts.'

'I won't give gifts every year. I just felt like giving them this year. I would like to give the gifts to your employees and not through you. Will you give me the list?'

'Sure, madam. I will do that.' And he disconnected the phone.

The manager called me again the next day. 'Madam, what gift are you planning to give my employees?'

'I know a good sari weaver and I don't have much time left now. So I will give a sari to everyone.'

'What about the men?'

'Every man has a woman at home. She could be a mother, wife, sister or daughter. He can give it to her. The sari is of very good quality.'

'Madam, men will be very upset with you. Women can wear your nice saris for the festival but the men won't have anything. I suggest you buy some pants and shirts material for them.'

I was tired of his interference. I said, 'Okay, let me think it over. We will talk later.'

The next day, he called me again. 'Madam, in our factory, there are tall people also. Should I send you the list separately so you can buy extra material for them?'

'Listen, I really don't have time for modifications. I won't be able to do that.'

'What colours are the saris and the material?'

'For the same price range, we will get different colours.'

'Oh, you can't do that. Some people may like the colour of their gift and others may not like it at all. So they may be very upset.'

'In that case, I will give the same colour to everybody.'

'No, madam, don't ever do that. They will think that you are giving them a uniform.'

'Then, what is your suggestion?' I said, exasperated.

'Maybe you can tell me your budget. Instead of you bringing the saris and the required material from Bangalore, I can buy them here in the village so that they can exchange it if they don't like the colour.'

I thought for a minute and said, 'No, that is not my policy.' I was fed up with him.

He continued, 'Okay, fine, madam, that is left to you. After all, you are the donor. Beggars are not choosers. However, I have a question. Who will pay for the stitching charges?'

'I am not paying.' I made it very clear.

'I am not paying either.' He made it even clearer.

He continued politely, 'So, may I suggest something different?'

'What is that?'

'If I give their sizes, you can buy stitched pants and shirts for the men.'

I was at the end of my tether but did not show it. I said, 'Send their measurements.'

My assistant, who had been overhearing the frequent calls said, 'Madam, why are you listening to him and his foolish options? After all, it is a gift.'

I said, 'I am not doing it for his sake. Most of the time, middle-level management do these things because they don't get such benefits or gifts. Ultimately, the poor people will suffer. The gift may not be a big sum for us. But each sari is precious to them. I am sure that they will treasure this sari and wear it for weddings. Unlike them, the manager's wife will buy expensive saris and won't even wear them. At the Foundation, we work for those people in whose life we can make a difference.'

Soon, it was the day to distribute the saris. I got the saris at one-third the price since I got them directly from the weaver. I got the two hundred saris packed and went to the factory. The men and women were standing in a queue happily waiting for their gifts. The manager was standing on one side and looked disapprovingly at me.

Before I gave the saris, I talked to the factory employees. 'My dear friends, I am giving this gift as a token of love and affection. It is coming from my heart. Diwali is an important festival and I want to celebrate it with your family by sharing whatever we have. There is a saying that when you get a gift, don't think of its price because it is the thought that is more important. So please don't worry about its price or colour. If anyone doesn't like the gift, you can return it to me and I will take it back.'

Then I started distributing the saris. I had not bought pants and shirts for anybody. All the men and women took the saris gracefully and happily. I saw that some of them even had tears in their eyes.

After the distribution, a man and a woman came to me and said, 'On behalf of everyone, we want to thank you. We have never seen such a wonderful gift in our twenty years of service. May God bless you. We may not be able to give you any gift but we wish you health and prosperity. Happy Diwali!'

I turned around and saw that there wasn't a single gift left for me to carry back.

12

The Gift of Sacrifice

During my tenure as a professor, Rajiv was one of my computer science students. Before ending each class, I told my students stories related to our country's history. Some students liked to hear them and some did not. Rajiv was not interested in history at all. So I asked him, 'Tell me your concept of history and how your generation thinks.'

He said, 'History is a dead subject of the past that gives us information about dead people and incidents. It is a chronology of events which is of no use today. I really feel that it is a waste of time.'

'Rajiv, when you go abroad for work or education, how do you interact with other people? How do you know what they say and what they mean and vice versa?' I asked.

'Oh, you should know the people with whom you interact.'

'If you want to know people, you should know the history of their land and where they come from. History also tells you about culture and culture is a big part of people's personalities.'

'How do you say that?'

'If you join me for one of my tours, I promise that, at the very least, you will be convinced that you need to keep an open mind.'

During one of my upcoming trips, I was planning to travel to a small town. There was a village near this town. Prakash, one of my ex-students, was now a senior manager in a software company and I knew that he was from that village. When Prakash learnt that I was travelling to the town, he called me up and said, 'Ma'am, instead of staying in the town, why don't you stay in my house in the village? It is only thirty kilometres away. My parents are staying alone there and they will be very happy to see you. Since you are interested in history, they will also take you around.'

I thought of Rajiv and asked him if he would like to come with me. Rajiv agreed and happily accompanied me.

I finished my work in the town and left for Prakash's village.

By the time we reached, it was evening but it was not dark. Prakash's father, Madappa, and mother, Parvati, were waiting for us. They said, 'Please relax at home. Our maid has made nice snacks for you. There is warm water in the bathroom. We will be back in an hour.'

I noticed that they were dressed to go out. They were ready with a thali containing a coconut, a garland, a diya and other small items, and I understood that they were going somewhere to perform a puja. I assumed they were going to a temple and said, 'Oh! If you are going to a temple, please wait a minute. I will change my sari and join you.'

Hesitantly, they said, 'It is not really a temple but it is like a temple to us. It is our family's worship site. Prakash might have told you about it.'

I could not contain my curiosity. 'Yes, Prakash told me that you will take me to a special historical place. Is this the same place?'

When they nodded, Rajiv also got ready and both of us accompanied them.

The worship site was at the outskirts of the village. There were fields all around us and we entered one of them. Green paddy was growing on all sides, but this field had only vegetables. There was a large neem tree in the field. Its shade covered most of the field. Below the tree, there was a large slab of stone standing on the ground. The lower part of the slab was buried deep in the soil.

There were many stone benches all around for people to come and relax here.

I noticed a tap in the corner. Madappa and Parvati washed their feet and face with tap water. With curiosity, Rajiv and I also did the same. Then Madappa took a jug of water and started washing the slab and Parvati got busy lighting a lamp nearby. I started paying attention to the details of the slab. It was approximately five and a half feet tall and two feet wide and the top looked like an arch. The slab had a beautiful border and its five horizontal compartments contained some amazing carvings.

The first compartment contained an inscription.

In the second compartment, on the right side, there was an image of a man with a sword sitting on a horse and, on the left, there was a man on foot who was only carrying a stick. I could see that the man with the stick was wearing a *veeragase*, which is a dress worn in villages. He had shoulder-length hair. He was angry and stood in a ready-to-attack position. There was an image of a cow behind him.

In the third compartment, four women with wings were flying with a palanquin while a man was sitting inside. I noticed the clouds in the background, the smile on the women's faces and their saris with waistbands.

In the fourth compartment, a man was sitting on a

throne. On either side were two women fanning him. The women wore jewellery and had tied their hair in a big bun. I could see the intricate designs of their bangles, chains, anklets and saris.

In the fifth and last compartment, there was an Ishwara Linga with a half-moon on one side and a sun on the other. There was a Nandi or bull in the front and a devotee was sitting with folded hands behind it.

'What is this? Why are you performing puja here?' asked Rajiv.

Madappa replied, 'This is a *veeragallu*, a stone that depicts valour. Gopala Golla, the cowherd, was our forefather. This is his story and his gift to us.'

'I don't understand,' said Rajiv.

Madappa did not talk further and started the puja. After the puja, we all sat on the benches and Madappa started telling us the story.

Gopala Golla was a young cowherd. He was around twenty-five years old and the only child to his parents. He had lost his father when he was very young. Gopala was recently married and his wife was pregnant. He was very happy with his ten cows. He liked to graze them near the hillock and enjoyed his peaceful life. One day, while he was playing the flute and grazing his cows, a soldier came riding on a horse. He stopped and dismounted from the horse. He gave Gopala Golla a silk cover and said, 'There is an urgent message inside. Enemies are following me. If you can go across the river and give this to the captain of our force, you will save the country. The captain is waiting below the neem tree. Since you are not a soldier, nobody will suspect that you are carrying this message.' Without waiting to hear back from Gopala, the solider mounted his horse and galloped away.

Gopala did not know what to do. He was a simple cowherd and did not know anything about how the kingdom was ruled or defended. But he knew one thing. Occasionally, enemy troops came and took away cows from the village. During these incidents, the king's soldiers came to protect the village and fought with the enemy troops. They were normally victorious.

Initially, Gopala thought about ignoring the soldier and doing nothing. He did not want to get into this mess. Then he thought that if he did not deliver the message, the enemy might win and occupy the kingdom. That would be much worse. Everyone would lose their cows and the enemies would burn the village. For the sake of the village and the cows, he decided to do what was necessary.

Gopala heard the sound of horses and immediately hid the silk cover in his lunch bag. A few minutes later, enemy soldiers came riding on horses and asked him, 'Did a soldier on a horse come this way?'

Gopala said, 'A soldier? Here? No, I haven't seen anyone except my cows.'

The enemy soldiers went away. Gopala took his lunch bag and started running towards the river, leaving his cows behind. He was not worried about them. He knew that when the sun went down, the cows would automatically go home.

Gopala's destination was a long distance away and the path was thorny. There was no road and he was worried that someone might follow him.

When he came to the river, he knew that he had to swim across. While he was getting ready to jump in, some enemy soldiers came out of the bushes and attacked him with their swords and javelins. Gopala only had a cowherd's stick, but he fought bravely and was seriously injured. He did not care about his injuries and jumped into the water. He crossed the river somehow and could barely walk once he reached the shore. He limped a short distance and then saw the neem tree. There he saw the captain waiting. Gopala gave the silk cover to him and then he fell to the ground and died.

The message that Gopala delivered was crucial in making an important decision during the battle.

Eventually, the king who ruled Gopala's village won. When the king learnt that a young lad had sacrificed his life without even being a soldier, he considered him to be a great martyr.

The king himself went to Gopala's house and consoled his old mother and pregnant young wife. He told Gopala's wife, 'Your loss is irreparable. Your husband sacrificed his life so that we can live in peace.' And he gave her a large piece of land exactly where Gopala had died.

Madappa paused and continued, 'We are his descendants. Over a period of time, we split the land and some of the descendants sold their portions. This portion has come to our family and I will keep it forever. Once a year, we have a festival in Gopala Golla's remembrance and all his descendants come to the village, no matter where they are. We assemble and conduct a puja for the stone. But Parvati and I come here every day to light a lamp for the great man.'

'Uncle, how did this stone come here and what do these figures mean?' asked Rajiv.

Madappa started explaining. 'This stone tells us Gopala's story. In the first section, it says that on this particular date, a king who ruled this area appreciated Gopala's martyrdom and gave the land as a gift to show respect for his sacrifice. His family will have sole ownership of this land.'

'How old is this inscription?'

'Around seven hundred years. The second section shows Gopala fighting with the soldiers. The third section shows that he died and the angels are taking him to his heavenly abode. The fourth section reveals that he has attained a great place in the court of warriors and is enjoying the luxuries there. Finally, the fifth section says that he is a great devotee of Ishwara. The half-moon and the sun indicate that this glory will last until the sun and moon exist. The stone was erected by the captain of the troop so that Gopala's sacrifice is remembered forever.'

'But who told you the story?' Rajiv asked. 'It is not written on the stone.'

'This story has been passed on from generation to generation in our family. Prakash also knows the story. It is his duty to pass it on to his children. If we didn't know the history of our family, then we would not know the value of this land and would have treated it like a commercial property.'

Now Rajiv looked at me and nodded his head. I knew that he had got his answer.

13

Bad Help

I was visiting the village I grew up in and was awaiting some papers from my office. Since the village was small, there was no courier service and the mail from my office had been sent by registered post. I went to the local post office and noticed that it was a small building with a skeletal staff. The building had not been renovated or painted in years. The fans were also not working because there was no electricity. The post office was hot and dusty. It was old and had very few customers because it had lost its importance due to the increased usage of email and Internet.

While waiting for my papers, I remembered my childhood. In our village, the postman was loved and highly respected. All of us at home waited for him. He was our main link to the outside world. He brought us greeting cards, parcels, money orders and letters. He distributed mail to the entire village. Our house was always his last stop of the day. He gave us our letters and then had lunch with us. During lunch, he told us lots of stories and gave us news from the village. The postman was like our personal news channel and we loved his visits. He also gave us financial advice and told us to buy government bonds and open a post-office savings account.

Today, I do not even go to the post office. I wondered, 'When I was younger, how did I correspond without email?'

I was brought back to reality when the postmaster said, 'It will take some time for us to get your papers. Why don't you go home? I will send the papers to you through my postman in the afternoon or evening.'

I replied, 'Thank you.' And I went home.

After lunch, a postman and a young boy came knocking at the door. The young boy was tall, handsome and reserved but his eyes were bright and shining. I invited them to sit down and offered them lunch. They refused politely.

The postman said, 'Ma'am, we have had lunch. Here are your papers. You need to sign for this. But . . .'

I signed the document and, without looking up, I asked him, 'What is it?'

He said, 'Meet my son, Satish. He is very intelligent. He has just finished his twelfth class with excellent marks. He has got admission in a prestigious engineering college called BITS Pilani . . .' And he stopped.

I looked at the boy. He looked uncomfortable with the conversation. His father continued, 'Ma'am, I can't afford his expenses at Pilani. I have never gone out of Karnataka. In fact, I have never even gone out of Dharwad district. He is my only child. I want him to be educated. You are from our village and you have seen the outside world. Is there any way you can help my boy study at BITS Pilani? With my salary, I can send him to the local engineering college but Satish is very keen to go outside.'

As a trustee of the Foundation, I immediately understood his situation. We come across many intelligent children who have high ambitions but an economically poor background. Most times, we help these children partially and sometimes we completely cover their educational expenses. This was one such case.

In a big city like Bangalore, there are many job opportunities; but in a small village, a postman only depends on his salary. I liked the boy and asked him for his marks card and admission letters. He was well prepared before he came to see me and showed me all the documents.

While browsing through the documents, I noticed that he had an interesting last name. When I asked him about it, Satish said, 'I have taken my last name from the name of my village.'

I told Satish, 'Well, I have everything I need right now. I promise that we will pay your first year's college fees and every year you have to send me your marks card. If you are on the merit list, we will continue paying your tuition until you complete your first degree.'

Satish and his father left the house with smiles on their faces. Every year, Satish's marks card came for our review and we sent money automatically. After four years, the marks card did not come and I knew that he must have completed his degree.

Many years passed and I forgot about Satish because he was one of the thousand recipients who had received help from the Infosys Foundation. We keep records of the recipients and the help we give them but we do not keep records of where they are, nor do they usually inform us.

I have a good friend, Vinita, who is from Maharashtra but lives in Bangalore. Her daughter was a software engineer working in a good company. Typical of an anxious parent, Vinita was searching for a suitable match for her daughter. She registered on bharatmatrimony.com, shaadi.com and many other sites. She also requested me to tell her if I knew someone suitable.

One day, I was visiting her neighbourhood and decided to drop in without calling ahead. It was 4 p.m. on a Sunday and I knew she would be at home. But when I entered, I realized that she had guests in her house. Vinita's daughter was dressed beautifully and she was talking to a young boy. His parents were sitting on a sofa. I understood that a young suitable groom had come to visit their house and talk to the girl.

I told Vinita, 'I am sorry. I should have called. I will come some other time.'

But Vinita did not let me go. She said, 'It doesn't matter. You are just like family. Come, sit down and join us.' So I did.

I looked at the boy's parents. They were fat and took up most of the large sofa. The father was in an expensive safari suit and wore a thick gold chain around his neck and sported a large gold ring. The mother had draped a very pricey Kanjeevaram sari around herself, and almost a quarter kilo of gold adorned her body. She wore a big bindi and plenty of flowers in her hair. I noticed that her hair was decorated with a *moggina male*, a small jasmine bud garland done in gold. She wore diamond *jhumki*s, dangling earrings which were not suitable for her age. The boy was tall and handsome. Despite the hot summer weather, he wore a costly suit, a gold kada and a diamond ring. From where I was sitting, I noticed that a luxurious car was waiting outside for them. I realized that they were extremely rich.

Compared to the boy and his family, Vinita's daughter herself was very simply dressed.

Vinita introduced me, 'Sudha is my old friend from college.' I folded my hands in a namaskara and, even though they reciprocated, I noticed immediately that they were uncomfortable. Before she could introduce them to me, I got a business call and went outside to take it. It turned out to be a long call.

By the time I returned, Vinita's guests were about to leave. The boy looked a bit pale. I smiled and said, 'I wish you all the best.' They left in a hurry.

Vinita and her daughter were very happy. She said, 'These people are very nice and come from a good family. The boy is a senior manager in a good company and owns an apartment in Jayanagar. His only sister is a software engineer. She is married and lives in America. The boy and his parents came last week to our house and liked our daughter. The boy wanted to come one more time. If all goes well, there may be an engagement as soon as next week. After that, the boy is going to America for a project. When he comes back, we will have the wedding. They want a big engagement and wedding—we don't have a problem with that.'

Vinita's husband entered the room. He said, 'Let's not talk about marriage and other details until they officially say yes. If they do so, next Thursday is a good day for the engagement.'

They all felt relaxed and nice about this matrimonial alliance.

I said, 'Sorry I got a call when you were about to introduce them to me. Tell me about this boy and his family.'

Vinita replied, 'We came in contact with them from the matrimonial sites on the Internet. The boy's name is Satish. He has also studied in the US, worked there for a few years and then he came back to India. His parents have been staying in Bangalore for the last five years. We did a background check on his education and job record and everything seems fine. He did his engineering from BITS Pilani. He was so intelligent that the institute even gave him a scholarship.'

BITS Pilani clicked in my mind because Satish was the only one who went to BITS Pilani from the list of people that we had helped through the Foundation. Most of the students that we funded were from Karnataka and went to local colleges.

I asked Vinita, 'What is Satish's last name?'

When Vinita told me his last name, it confirmed my suspicion, but I did not want to say anything to her until I had verified our records. 'When did he complete his education at BITS?' I asked.

Vinita gave me the year and said, 'Right now, he is thirty years old. He finished his degree when he was twenty-two. What did you think of the boy?'

I told her, 'I don't know. I have only met him once. But he looks good.'

Vinita insisted, 'You must come for the engagement.'

I replied, 'Of course. Kindly confirm the date at the earliest.' And I left.

The next day, I went to my office and checked our records. It was indeed the same Satish. I was very happy that he had done well for himself. Now I understood why his parents wore so much gold and showed off their wealth. It was because they came from a deprived background and had recently acquired wealth. So they went overboard buying things that they could never afford before.

I picked up the phone to call Vinita and tell her I

knew the family and that the boy was very intelligent. But something stopped me. I thought, 'Why didn't they recognize me? Why didn't they even acknowledge me? At the Foundation, we do not expect gratitude from everybody but it is normal to at least expect some courtesy.'

As I worked backwards, I realized what might have happened. Satish and his family may not have told Vinita's family about their background. They had probably also hidden the fact that Satish's father was once a postman. They wanted to show Vinita and her family that they had always been rich. I was not sure whether I should tell Vinita. There is nothing wrong in being poor; and if people want to hide their background, it is left to their value system. I should not be judgemental about that.

While my mind was oscillating between whether I should make the phone call or not, the phone rang. It was Vinita. She sounded sad. She said, 'Sorry, there is no engagement. The boy doesn't want to marry our daughter.'

'Why? What happened?' I asked.

'I have no idea. They were so enthusiastic about the wedding until their visit on Sunday. I don't know why they changed their mind.'

I kept quiet. I wanted to be completely sure before I told Vinita anything. 'What is their background? What does the father do?' I asked.

'The father is a landlord. They own properties in a village in North Karnataka and they come from generations of family wealth. You are from the same area. Have you ever heard of them?'

'Yes, Vinita, I know them. I didn't want to say anything until I was absolutely sure. Satish's father was a postman and the boy is very bright. We helped with Satish's education through the Foundation but he has accomplished everything on his own. They must have thought that I recognized them and would tell you the truth. So they backed out of the engagement. That is my reading of the situation.'

I finished the call and kept sitting, busy with my thoughts. I had never thought that getting an economic need based scholarship would bring shame to Satish and his family. That was the reason he had refused to recognize me. For the first time in my life, I understood that if a person is not comfortable with the help given to him, it becomes a lifelong burden for him to carry.

14

Sharing with a Ghost

Two decades ago, I was teaching in a college. The campus was so large that only half the area was occupied by the college, while the other half was taken up by the primary section of a high school. I was chairperson of the prize committee of our college. A philanthropist had left some money to the college for a prize to be given to the student who got the highest marks in the Kannada language. The prize money of one thousand rupees was always given on College Day.

The job of the clerk in the prize committee was to go through all the marks cards of the final-year students and give the list of prizewinners to the committee. In those days, there was no computer scanning, automatic sorting or email. The clerk had to manually prepare the list.

That year, Rohini got eighty-five marks in Kannada. That was the highest in the college. We announced her name as prizewinner on the college noticeboard. The next day, Rohini came to my office. She said, 'Ma'am, there is a mistake. Sunita, who is studying in Section D, has also got eighty-five marks.'

'How do you know?' I asked her.

'Sunita told me to collect her marks card on her behalf. So I came to the office and noticed that she had the same marks as me. But on the noticeboard, only my name was displayed. There must be some error. So I came to tell you.'

I was happy about Rohini's honesty. I immediately called the clerk and asked him about Sunita's marks. Shyly, he said, 'Sorry, madam, I mistook eighty-five for thirty-five, hence the error.'

Firmly, I asked him to get his eyes tested the next day so that this mistake was not repeated. If Rohini had not informed me, the college would have been unfair to a meritorious student.

Rohini happily shared her money with Sunita on College Day.

Sharing reminds me of many other interesting incidents I encountered while at the college.

Once I was interviewing people for a position. My colleague on the interview board said, 'When the merits of the candidates are equal, we should select a person who plays cricket rather than tennis.' I was surprised at this comment. I had always thought that both cricket and tennis were just games. When I looked at him, he explained, 'Cricket teaches us to share success but tennis teaches us individualism.'

One rainy day, I was looking at the primary section of the school from my office. It was drizzling. I saw a young mother with a big umbrella. She had come to pick up her little girl from school. This little girl wanted to share the umbrella with her friend who did not have one. Even though the mother knew that they could share, she told the little girl, 'Look darling, I only have one umbrella. Let her bring her own umbrella. Two of you cannot share one.' I felt that the mother should have encouraged her child to share. It would have been an important lesson in life.

In another incident on Children's Day (14 November), a teacher called me to conduct games in the primary school. We made three groups of ten students each, gave five bananas to each group and asked them to share the fruits among themselves. The results were startling. The first group had five aggressive children. They took a banana each and the remaining five children were left with none. In the second group, three children shared two bananas and seven children shared the remaining three. In the third group, all ten of them shared the five bananas equally. The worst thing was that the mothers of the aggressive children in the first group were extremely happy and congratulated each other, 'Oh, my child is very smart and super-competitive. I am sure that this is the right attitude in the modern age.' I was disillusioned when I realized that the mothers who were supposed to inculcate good moral values in their children had never taught them to share.

In this context, Rohini sharing her prize money made me very happy indeed.

When I was teaching the final-year students, I gave my class an assignment with a time limit of one day. The earliest and first correct submission would get the highest marks. One of my students, Priya, was quite brilliant. I expected her to finish first but she did not. She submitted the assignment with everyone else. I asked Priya to stay back after class and asked her, 'Priya, why did you take so much time? It was not a difficult assignment for a person like you.' With sadness in her voice, she said, 'Ma'am, my assignment was complete and ready last night itself but, when I came to the computer lab, someone had stolen the cable connecting the computer to the common shared printer so I couldn't take a printout. In our college, we don't have individual printers because it is expensive. We use one printer which is shared by all students of the same batch. It reduces our costs and we learn to share. When I came today, the cable was connected. Everybody took printouts and so did I.' I realized that the culprit could have been a jealous classmate who was too lazy to do the assignment early and wanted to delay others by not sharing the printer.

Sharing is an important quality that binds people, and society itself survives on sharing. I always tell the following story to my students in class before I teach management decision-making.

A long, long time ago, an ordinary person was born into a very intellectual family in a village. Everybody looked down upon him because he was not accomplished. He was the black sheep of the family. Unable to bear the insults, he left home and decided to end his life. When he reached the next village, he saw a big abandoned house on the outskirts. He thought that he would spend his last night there.

A passer-by saw him entering the gates of the abandoned house and said, 'Young man, it is getting dark. Are you planning to spend the night there? Are you mad? There is a ghost inside that house. That is why nobody stays there. Take my advice and get out.'

The young man thought that this was perfect. It was

best that the ghost killed him so that he did not even have to plan his death.

Darkness descended as the night drew closer. The young man waited for the ghost.

Suddenly, a voice from somewhere said, 'Young man, why are you here? Are you not scared of me?'

Without getting perturbed, the young man replied, 'I know you are here. Still, I want to stay.'

The ghost was shocked at the reply. Normally, people ran away from him but this man was not scared. So the ghost asked, 'Why have you come here?'

The young man explained his situation.

After listening to the young man, the ghost inquired, 'Are you ready to learn, work hard, do your homework and practise whatever you learn? If so, I will teach you the Sanskrit language including grammar and its great works.'

The young man agreed. So the ghost and the young man started their classes as teacher and student.

Day after day, the young man continued to learn. Months rolled by and years passed. The young man never saw the ghost and only heard his voice. One day, the ghost suddenly appeared in front of him and said, 'Young man, you have now mastered the language. Will you allow me to go to heaven?'

The young man was perplexed, 'When did I stop

you from going to heaven? Who are you? Why did you teach me?'

The ghost sighed and shared his story. 'I was an extremely learned and rich man in this town. This is my mansion. I never shared my knowledge or my money with anyone. I was scared that if I gave away knowledge, then some smart person may become better than me. If I distributed my wealth, I thought that I might become poor. I wanted to remain a learned and powerful man and I died without sharing. When my soul went to heaven, I was thrown back as a ghost to my own mansion with an instruction that until I taught someone, shared my knowledge sincerely and distributed my wealth, I would not attain heaven and would remain a ghost. I could distribute money very easily but not my knowledge. People were so scared of me that they never came and stayed here. I had been waiting for a good and eager student for several years. Then you came here. Whatever I knew, I have taught you. You have helped me attain my salvation. I thank you and now I want to go. Please remember the parting words of your teacher—in life, sharing is important.'

Many years later, this young man became a great critic of the poet Kalidasa. Thanks to him, we have much knowledge about the great poet. The young man's name was Bharavi.

15

Foot in the Mouth

Savitri was a lecturer, a colleague of mine during my teaching days. She was sharp and came from a rich background. She loved to spend her time gossiping about people instead of doing any constructive work. All our colleagues knew about her nature and, as an inside joke, the teachers called her Savitri G, where 'G' stood for 'Gossip'.

People who did not know her realized very soon that she had a knack of creating news out of nothing. After that, they avoided her and, in the end, Savitri was always lonely. So she was always on the lookout for people who would sit with her and gossip.

One day, I accidentally ran into her in the college canteen. Before I could go the other way, she saw me and caught hold of my hand so tightly that even Superman could not have loosened the grip. I did not want to create a scene in front of my students, who consider us role models. So we settled down at a table for a cup of coffee.

Almost immediately, the college bell rang for the next class. I wanted to get out of her clutches, so I lied and said, 'Savitri, I have a class now. I will see you later.'

I got up. She asked, 'Which class are you taking and in which room?'

Lying spontaneously is not my strength and, when we lie, we have to remember the untruths we have fabricated. It is hard work to lie. I said the first thing that came to my mind, 'Room Number 207.'

'Which class?' she asked.

I replied, 'First year MCA students.'

Smiling victoriously, she said, 'Learn how to lie properly. Today, the first year MCA class has gone on a picnic with their class teacher Ganesh.'

I was still trying to escape her clutches and I said, 'Sorry, I meant second year MCA.'

'Keep quiet and sit down. Rooms 201 to 210 have been getting whitewashed since yesterday.'

I knew I was guilty and I had no other option but to sit down again.

Savitri started talking immediately. It felt as if she had been in solitude for months and had found a listener after a long time.

'What is the latest news?'

'Well, there is this latest scam. Also, there is so much traffic in Bangalore.'

Sarcastically, Savitri replied, 'I also read newspapers and see TV, you know. I wasn't talking about that kind of news.' She paused, then continued, 'Have you heard the rumours about Anusuya? I just couldn't believe what I heard.'

Anusuya or Ansi as I called her was a common friend. She was dignified and non-interfering. I was a little worried when Savitri started talking in a hush-hush manner about her. I asked, 'Why? What happened to Ansi?'

'Do you know that there is some problem in her marriage? Ansi and Girish are separated.'

'How do you know that?'

'Whenever I call Ansi, she always says that her husband is abroad or travelling. Tell me, isn't that unusual?'

'No, it isn't. Girish is in a senior position at work and he has to travel a lot. What is wrong in that? And whenever you might have called, he must have been travelling. I met Girish only yesterday.'

'Oh, really? Who was with him?' Savitri shot questions at me like a detective.

'He was at the Taj West End with one of his lady colleagues.'

I saw that Savitri was bubbling with excitement. I regretted the words the moment they came out of my mouth. I did not want to give Savitri any more ammunition.

'Well, don't stop. How old was she?'

'I didn't ask for her birth certificate.' Now I was really annoyed at myself and at her.

'Cool down. Was she in her mid-twenties or in her thirties?'

'I don't know. Girish had a business meeting and there were many people around them. I didn't find anything amiss. Don't you attend seminars with our male colleagues? How would you feel if someone talked about you like that? Savitri, please, let us not gossip.'

But she was not listening to me at all. She continued as if I had not said anything, 'These days, with make-up, even a forty-five-year-old woman looks like she's twenty-five. So maybe that's why you weren't able to guess her age. If I were you, I would have rightly guessed it and immediately informed Ansi to take care of her husband. Cautioning people is also a form of social work. Anyway, you won't understand.'

She changed the topic and without waiting for my answer, she asked, 'Have you met Roma lately?'

Roma was another common friend. She was very

fashionable and had a modern outlook. I knew that Roma was a good woman.

Savitri continued her commentary, 'Money has gone to Roma's head. How can her husband earn so much money in such a short period? They must be doing something illegal. Without working hard, they have made so much money. Look at Roma. She is so fashionable. She wears only designer saris and can be seen in beauty parlours getting expensive facials. She even has a personal fitness trainer. She doesn't help her poor relatives at all but is ready to spend a lot of money on herself.'

'How do you know all this?'

She smiled and said, 'I don't talk without proof. Govind told my driver.'

'Who is Govind?'

'Govind is my driver's friend and Roma's driver's cousin.'

I did not know what Govind had told Savitri's driver and how Savitri had interpreted it. But I knew Roma well. It was true that Roma was fashionable and rich, but that did not mean that she did not help others. Roma had come to our Foundation office many times to give a cheque with a large amount of money as donation. She always requested me not to tell anyone about it. I also knew that all of Roma's relatives had built houses with her help and even bought cars but nobody said it in public because Roma never wanted people to know. She liked to donate anonymously. We should never judge a person from the outside. But there was no point in talking about these things to Savitri, who would just gossip and find a reason to blame others without even knowing the details.

I got irritated with Savitri and was about to get up. Savitri again changed the subject. 'Sumati is a fine lady and very innocent too. I consider innocence and ignorance the same. What do you think?'

Sumati was very calculative, shrewd and not a reliable friend. Sumati's own sisters had told me many stories about her. They said that she pretended to be very simple and behaved as if she was very innocent and principled. She was working in a government department and had been suspended once because she had been caught engaging in malpractice.

Thankfully, the bell rang, and I was glad that this one hour was over.

I got up and firmly said, 'Savitri, don't judge a person by their looks or from rumours. Looks can be deceptive. It is not that all rich people are bad and neither is it true that all simple-looking people are innocent. Ignorance is different from innocence. Ignorance is a lack of knowledge but innocence is about trust and believing other people. A child is always innocent but we adults are ignorant and hardly innocent. Savitri, gossip is bad and spoils many families. When you talk about somebody, remember that someone somewhere is also talking about you. People might like to hear gossip to pass time but everybody dislikes a gossipmonger. Eventually, they want to keep such people at a distance.'

Even as I said the words, I understood that they would not get into Savitri's head. She was now looking at our colleague Kamala, who was settling down with her cup of coffee at a table near us. Without even bidding me goodbye, Savitri got up and moved to Kamala's table. I knew that I would be the next target in her gossip sessions. I had put my foot in my mouth.

16

Miserable Success

Vishnu was a young, bright and ambitious student from the first batch I ever taught at college. So my relationship with him was closer than that with my students from subsequent batches. He was charming, communicative and clear in his thinking.

In college, we used to have long arguments on different issues and we used to agree to disagree on many matters. I used to tell Vishnu, 'Vishnu, I have seen many more seasons than you. With my experience in life, I want to tell you that having good relationships, compassion and peace of mind is much more important than achievements, awards, degrees or money.'

Vishnu would argue back, 'Madam, your stomach is full and you have achieved everything. Hence, you are comfortable in life and can say that. You have received many awards, so you don't care for them and you are not ambitious. You will never understand people like me.' Then, I usually just smiled at him. I liked him for his openness.

Vishnu was also very good at teaching. He completed his degree and got an excellent job in Microsoft in Seattle, USA. He was awaiting his visa to go abroad. I told him to teach at my college while he was waiting. Whenever I could not attend the laboratory sessions, I told him to take charge of the junior lab and be my substitute. He became very popular with the students.

I asked Vishnu, 'You are very good at teaching, why don't you seriously think of becoming a professor?'

He said, 'My monthly salary in the USA is more than a teacher's annual salary here. Why would I want to become a professor?'

'Vishnu, don't be so rude. A teacher is not respected for the salary but for his or her knowledge and teaching. If you don't respect the teaching profession, that is fine but don't make such a comparison.'

Soon, Vishnu left the country on his new assignment.

Many years passed and a decade rolled by. My students, who were once young, were now middle-aged and I had gone from middle age to old age.

One day, my secretary told me that someone called Vishnu wanted to meet me. By this time, I knew many

Vishnus and was not able to place him at once. She said that he was a student from my first batch of students. Now I recognized him instantly and told her to set up an appointment. After all, old wine, old memories and old students are precious in life.

On the day of the appointment, Vishnu walked in right on time. He had less hair than before and some of them were grey. He had put on weight. He was wearing an expensive shirt and there was a platinum diamond ring on his finger. But alas, his face was like a dried tomato. There was not a trace of enthusiasm on it. On the contrary, I could see some lines of worry on his face.

He sat in front of me and I ordered him a cup of tea. Vishnu looked at me and said, 'Madam, you look really old now.'

I smiled and said, 'Time and tide will wait for no one.' But he did not smile back. 'How are you, Vishnu?' I asked. 'I haven't met you for fifteen years. It is very nice of you to remember your old teacher and come to see me. Where are you? What are you doing now? Are you still with Microsoft?'

'No, madam. I left Microsoft after three years,' replied Vishnu.

'No wonder people say that if someone stays in a software company for more than three years, he is a loyal person!'

He did not respond to my joke. 'So where are you now?' I asked again.

'I own a company in Singapore. Two hundred people work for me. We make very good profit.' I felt Vishnu's voice had that pride of achievement, which was very natural.

'So you have settled in Singapore?'

'Not really, I come to India quite often because of work. I have a house in Vasant Vihar in Delhi, a flat in Worli in Mumbai, a bungalow in Raj Mahal Vilas Extension in Bangalore, a farm on Bannerghatta Road . . .'

I stopped him. 'Vishnu, I didn't ask you about your assets. I am not an income tax person. I just wanted to know where you normally stay.' I was pulling his leg, yet he did not smile.

'Vishnu, you have told me enough of your financial assets,' I continued. 'Now tell me about your marital status. Are you married? How many children do you have? What do they do?' Usually, a mother and a teacher get the automatic authority to pose these questions to her children and students. I am no exception. Some people mind my questions because it is their personal life and I get the hint and stop. But most people happily tell me about their life.

'Yes, I am married. I have an eight-year-old daughter,' he said.

Vishnu pulled out his wallet and showed me his family photo. When he was in college, he used to go out with Bhagya, a girl junior to him. But the lady in the photograph was different. She was stunningly beautiful, like a model, and his daughter was cute.

I felt that his life was a picture perfect postcard. He was successful, rich, had a very pretty wife and a daughter. What else can one want in life? With this kind of success, he should be very happy and enthusiastic—but he was not. I did not know the reason, but I knew that he would tell me. I stopped talking and allowed Vishnu to speak.

Slowly, Vishnu opened up. 'Madam, I have a problem. I have come to talk to you.'

'What problem? And why do you think I have the solution? Actually, a successful person like you should help an old teacher like me,' I joked to reduce the tension.

'It is nothing to do with success, madam. For the last few years, I have been feeling very sad. I feel like I am missing something in life. I can't pinpoint exactly what it is,' he said. 'Nothing makes me happy. Nothing even moves me or touches my heart, even if I see a heart-wrenching incident. I feel that I am travelling in a desert without water and the roads are paved with gold and silver . . .'

I asked him directly, 'Have you seen a doctor or a counsellor?'

'Of course I have. They said that a compassionate heart is important to enjoy life. They told me to read books and advised me to try and be happy by doing things such as looking at the sunrise, listening to the birds, taking long walks and exercising regularly.'

'Well, what happened?'

'I lost weight with all the activities but otherwise things didn't improve. I went back to a counsellor again. He told me to go to Somalia on a trip.'

'Why Somalia?' I was surprised. 'I know that there are trips to Europe, Hong Kong and Bangkok. But I have never heard of a trip to Somalia. Tell me, did you go there? What did you do in Somalia?' I was curious.

'Oh, they took us to orphanages, HIV camps and camps of children suffering from malnutrition. But nothing happened. I still didn't feel anything. On the contrary, my mind was busy calculating how Somalia could export to America or other European nations. What would you have done in my place, madam?' he questioned me.

'Don't put me in your shoes. What I would do is left to me and you don't have to do the same thing. Why can't you talk to someone who is very dear to you—maybe a friend or your wife or someone from your age group? They might be able to give you a better solution. After all, there is a generation gap between us.'

He was quiet. Then he said, 'Madam, all my life, I have calculated and made friendships. I have never spent time with people who aren't useful to me in some way. After all, life is a merciless, competitive field. Every move should take me one step higher on the ladder of success.'

I thought to myself, 'Now I know why Bhagya was replaced by the model wife.'

'How much time do you spend with your family?'

'My daughter is friendly but she is nice to me only when she wants something from me. Sometimes, I find it very strange. A child looks beautiful only with innocence but my daughter is more practical. My wife is very busy with the carpet business that she inherited from her father. She doesn't have any time to talk to me and my daughter even though she works from home most of the time.'

He stopped for a second and continued, 'Or maybe I think that way. My wife wants to get all my contacts and clients so that she can expand her business. I am more of a database to her than a companion.'

I understood Vishnu's problem. Sometimes, it is very difficult to talk with your own family. I was touched that he felt safe coming to me. But he was expecting a quick fix from me. I was willing to listen to his problem, but that did not mean that I also knew the solution.

Vishnu continued, 'Madam, tell me, how do I become compassionate? How do I build a strong family? How can I enjoy the sunrise and the moonlight? How much time does it take to get all these qualities? Are there any books or a crash course or people who can teach me? I don't care about the cost but it shouldn't take months together.'

I was shocked by his approach. 'Vishnu, compassion cannot be taught, sold or bought,' I said. 'There is no time limit either. It is one of the characteristics that you have to develop from the beginning. Understand that life is a journey. In that short journey, if you can show compassion to others, show it now. Our ancestors have always talked about the middle path for a reason. That path makes a person stable, happy and content. Vishnu, you are the role model for your children. Children will be what they see. What you have done, your daughter has copied.'

Vishnu sighed and said, 'Yes, madam. I understand what you are saying. I will take my daughter and work with poor people on a regular basis along with her. That will also help us bond. I am hoping that it will make me a better human being and I will be able to feel worthy again. Now I know what brought me to you. I cannot thank you enough.'

Vishnu left my office with hope in his heart and a smile on his face.

17

Shraddha

My father, Dr R.H. Kulkarni, passed away twelve years ago. He was a doctor and a professor of gynaecology in a medical college. He always believed that education for women is essential. So he sent me to an engineering college in 1968. It was a time when most girls' fathers could not even dream of doing that because of societal pressures. My father loved his daughters and son equally and had the same rules for all his children. He even divided his assets equally among all of us.

My father's *shraddha* occurs on 30 October every year. Suresh was my father's favourite nephew and he always performed my father's memorial service. I kept money in a fixed deposit account and the interest accruing from this was used to meet the shraddha expenses in a temple nearby. Every year, our family went to the temple, watched my cousin Suresh perform the shraddha and had lunch together. Then, in the evening, I went to an orphanage and gave fruits to the children. We had been following this routine for the past eleven years.

Last year, however, Suresh was in Paris on work at the end of October and he was not available to perform the shraddha. But, as usual, my family and I went to the temple. I sat on the bench waiting for the manager.

I saw my friend Meera at the temple. She seemed worried. I asked her, 'What's happened?'

'My brother, Murali, has not reached here yet. Today is my mother's shraddha. I want it to be performed here because Murali said that this temple was near his new house.'

I knew Meera's family very well and was surprised by her answer. 'Why has Murali shifted to a new house?' I asked. 'What happened to your old house?'

Meera's mother had been a schoolteacher. She had saved every penny of her salary and pension and built a nice house. She was extremely fond of her home and called it 'Sarthaka' (which means fulfilment). She died a few years ago. Meera had already lost her father when she was a child. Her mother had single-handedly raised Meera and her brother.

With sadness, Meera replied, 'As you know, Murali got into bad company. He had loans to repay, so he sold the house. Now he has rented a house near this temple. Yesterday, I went and begged him to come early to perform our mother's shraddha. I am even paying the entire cost for this ceremony.'

I fell silent and started looking around. There was an older lady sitting near us and she seemed worried as well. She kept looking at her watch and glancing at the door. Casually, I asked her, 'Are you waiting for somebody?'

'Yes, I am waiting for my son. He is a senior manager in a software company. Today is the release date of his project. He said that he would be here by this time. His cellphone is switched off and I don't know what has happened. If he doesn't show up, how will we perform my husband's shraddha? I am very concerned.'

I realized that three women were sitting on a bench waiting to perform shraddha for their loved ones. The temple manager came and asked us for the names of the people for whom we wanted to perform shraddha. All three of us promptly gave the names. Then he said proudly, 'Shraddha is a religious ceremony, which is very important for the family. Today, the deceased, his or her father and forefather, that is, three generations of people, come down to earth in the form of the cow, the sun and God. When a family member gives *til* seeds and water, your remembrance reaches them. Shraddha is a ceremony that must be performed with shraddha or devotion.'

He looked at us and said, 'Where are the male members of your families? Call them now. Tell them to get ready. I will arrange three pundits to help them.'

Then he sat on a chair and started sorting through receipts.

I replied, 'Sir, at this moment, we don't have any male members from our families.'

'Then I will call a helper from the kitchen. He will perform the shraddha on your families' behalf.'

For a second, I stopped. Then, firmly, I said, 'No, sir. I can perform my father's shraddha. I don't need an unknown male to perform shraddha for someone he doesn't even know.'

The manager continued to sort through receipts. He did not even bother to look at me before answering, 'Sorry, madam. No woman can perform shraddha for anyone. This is the rule. If you cannot accept that, then just have lunch here, pray to God and go home.'

'No, sir, I can't accept your decision,' I said. 'After all, this is my father's shraddha. As a daughter, I have the right to remember my father today. It is my duty too. Is there any book that says that a woman can't perform shraddha and that only male members are allowed to do so?'

The manager stopped sorting receipts and looked at me. He was taken aback by my answer. He could not believe what he was hearing. He said, 'It is a tradition.'

'Sorry, sir. Tradition is different from ritual. A tradition passes down values to the next generation but a ritual or ceremony is what you do by practice and habit. For example, performing shraddha is a tradition, but the fact that it is done by a man is a ritual. We shouldn't break traditions but rituals can be changed depending on the circumstances. Rituals are almost always formed based on geographical, economic and social conditions.'

The manager was not happy with my argument. 'Listen, madam,' he said patiently. 'We have never allowed a woman to perform shraddha before. No woman has ever questioned our procedures till now.'

'If it hasn't been done before, you can start today,' I said. 'Every journey starts with a single step. I don't think that it is wise to perform rituals without understanding them. My father used to tell me a story. There was a person who used to perform puja every day and a cat used to trouble him during his puja. So, he told his son, "Tie the cat and give it some milk every day when I do puja." The cat never troubled him again. After a few years, both the man and the cat died. The son took over and started performing the puja. Since the cat had died, he brought the neighbour's cat, tied it and poured milk for the cat every day during puja time. The son had never understood why his father had asked him to give milk to the cat every day. It had become a meaningless ritual. You are doing the same thing.'

By this time, a crowd had formed around us and people were listening to our argument. The manager said, 'But, madam, how can a woman perform shraddha?'

'Why can't she? When I wrote out a cheque for this temple, you accepted it. You never checked whether it came from a man or a woman. In the olden days, there was a division of labour between men and women because large families stayed together. That is why men worked outside the home and women inside. Today, women work equally well in all fields. There is no difference. If you don't allow me to perform shraddha, you are establishing a fact that no daughter can perform her father's shraddha and no wife can perform her husband's shraddha. Just because she is a female, does it mean that a woman has no feelings towards her brother, father or husband? That is unfair. I am going to perform shraddha today, come what may.'

The manager was amused by my insistence and said, 'If that is so, we don't have any pundit who will be willing to help you perform shraddha.'

The crowd stayed silent and nobody took any sides. There were also many young and old pundits listening to us. I looked at them, 'Is there anyone who can help me?'

Some young priests smiled at me but did not step forward. To my surprise, an old man said, 'I will help you perform your father's shraddha.' I knew that this man was the most senior in the temple. Softly, he continued, 'I have seen sons who talk on their phones while performing shraddha. Their mind is never on the ceremony. I have seen men who go out, smoke, come back and continue the ceremony. I have seen men who tell me that they will give me more money if I complete the ceremony in five minutes. Then there are others who do it with love and remembrance. But when men who are not interested can perform shraddha, why should a woman who is sincerely pleading be denied? As per the tradition, we believe that the ancestors come down to earth on the day of the shraddha and they should not go back empty-handed.'

I felt relieved and turned back. I saw that Meera and the older lady wanted to say something. Meera said, 'I also want to perform my mother's shraddha.'

The older lady said, 'I just got a call from my son and he says that he is stuck in a traffic jam. Never mind, I will perform my husband's shraddha too.'

The old man gave each of us a *dharba* ring made of dry straw, black til and water. Then he said, 'Come in. Let us start.'

I am sure my father loved the shraddha that year. I could feel my father, grandfather and great-grandfather smiling down at me proudly.

After the ceremony, I thought to myself, 'With age, I was wondering if I had started accepting a male-dominated society—but now I know that it isn't true. No wonder I wrote that letter to J.R.D. Tata in 1974.'

18

Lazy Portado

Portado was a young, bright, handsome and sweet boy from Goa. We were in BVV College of Engineering at Hubli. He had been my classmate and lab partner throughout our course. So I knew him fairly well.

Portado had peculiar habits. Though he was intelligent, he was extremely lazy. Our theory classes were from eight in the morning till noon and lab was from two to five in the afternoon. Portado never came for the first class at eight. Occasionally, he turned up for the second or third hour but most of the time he only showed up for the last hour. He never missed our lab sessions, however.

In those days, attendance was not compulsory in college and our teachers were very lenient. They requested Portado to come on time but since there was no internal assessment, they couldn't really exercise their authority.

One day, I asked Portado, 'Why are you always late? What do you do at home?'

He laughed and said, 'I have a lot of things to do. I am so busy in the evenings that I can't get up before nine in the morning.'

'What things keep you so busy?' I asked him innocently.

'I meet my friends at night. We have long chats followed by dinner. You know, it takes a lot of time to build friendships. You will not understand. You people are all nerds. You only come to college to study.'

'Portado, you are a student. You should study, get knowledge, learn skills and work hard. Is that not important?'

'Oh, please. You remind me of my mother. Don't give me a sermon. Life is long. We have plenty of time. We should not learn anything in a hurry. We shouldn't be so stingy about time either.'

Then I noticed that he did not even have a watch since, for obvious reasons, he had no need for it.

Portado continued, 'In life, you need connections and networking. That can give you success. You can't network in a day. You have to spend time and money on building a network. Who knows? Some people that I meet now may make it big tomorrow and then that connection will work for me.'

I was a young girl from a middle-class and academic-minded family. I believed only in hard work. I never understood how networking could help.

During our college breaks, Portado proudly told us about his childhood, 'Oh, when I was young, I spent my time in big cities like Bombay, Delhi and Calcutta. In Calcutta, there are so many clubs. It is a matter of prestige to be a member of a club. When I start working, I want to be a member of all the good clubs in the city.' Every now and then, Portado felt that Hubli was a small and boring town. So he regularly went to Belgaum to meet his friends and 'network' with them.

During exams, Portado worked like a donkey. He glass-traced most of my original drawings so that he did not have to think about the solutions to engineering problems himself. His glass trace drawings were definitely better than the originals because they were neater and there were no wrinkles or pencil marks. He always got more than me in drawings. He even kept the question papers of previous years and made his own question papers by process of elimination. Instead of reading textbooks, he read guides to pass the exams. With all this, he always managed to pass in second class.

Once the examiner caught him because in a survey drawing he told the examiner that the mark on his drawing was actually a big tree in the middle of a road. It was a survey of a town near Dharwad. Unfortunately, the examiner happened to be from that town and he knew that there was no tree on that road. He questioned Portado, who said with a serious face, 'Sir, I have done the survey myself. I sat below the tree, had my lunch and then I continued.'

Calmly, the examiner said, 'I can't see this tree in any of your classmates' original drawings. This is only a mosquito between the glass and the drawing that you have tried to cover up.'

Portado just managed to pass the exams that year. But he was not perturbed. He said, 'I am not scared of the exams or the marks. Today's nerds will be tomorrow's mid-level managers. A person with good networking will be their boss.'

Because of his attitude and undisciplined habits, even the college hostel refused to keep him. So he rented a small house near college and lived there like a king.

Once our class planned a picnic trip to Belgaum. Since Portado was familiar with the city, we decided to take his opinion and help. The picnic committee members, including myself, went to his house around eleven on a Sunday morning. We all assumed that Portado would be awake. But to our surprise, he was still in bed. When he opened the door, he said sleepily, 'Oh, why have you come so early on a Sunday?' He was quite annoyed to see us. 'Well, I am awake now, so please come in.'

We went in but there was absolutely no place to sit. His clothes were all over the room and newspapers were scattered on the floor. In the kitchen, the dirty dishes were piled up in the sink and they were stinking. There were fish bones everywhere. There was also a cat and a dog inside the house. They were well fed with Portado's leftovers. The windows were not open either. The bedsheet looked like it had not been changed for a year. I did not have the courage to go see his bathroom.

Portado felt neither perturbed nor guilty. He said, 'Make some space for yourselves and sit down.' Some people moved Portado's undergarments and made some space but I could not do that because I was a girl, so I simply stood. Portado brought a stool for me from his kitchen. It was very sticky. I was even more hesitant to sit on it than on his clothes. I told him, 'It is better that I stand.' Portado offered us tea but none of us had the guts to drink any.

When I asked him about planning the details of the picnic, he said, 'We can start at twelve in the afternoon. My friend owns a lodge so I can take you there. The next day, we can go to Amboli Falls. Then we can also go to

Goa.' Portado made a ten-day programme. But most of us could not afford a ten-day accommodation in a hotel, nor could we skip class for so many days. So the plan fizzled out. We thanked him and left. When I turned back and looked, Portado had closed the door and had probably gone back to bed.

Soon the final year came around. We all passed the examinations and parted ways. Some of us felt sad because we had become a big family in the last four years together. We did not know our destinations and knew that we may not meet again. Of course, as Portado said goodbye he told us, 'If you are ever in Goa, please come to my house.' But I seriously doubted that I would ever run into him again.

Many decades passed. Once I went to Dubai to give a lecture. After the lecture, people came up to talk to me but there was one person who waited until everybody had left. Then he walked over to where I was sitting and smiled. I recognized the smile but I did not remember where I had seen him. The man was bald, fat, had a big paunch and was dressed very ordinarily. I thought that he might be a mid-level manager in a construction company. I meet many people in my field and it is difficult to remember everybody.

I asked him, 'What can I do for you, sir? Are you waiting for me?'

With a cracked voice, he said, 'Yes, I have been waiting for you for a long time.'

'Oh, I'm sorry, I didn't know that you were waiting. Do you have any work with me?' I said.

'Yes, I just wanted to tell you that you were right and I was wrong.'

I was puzzled. What did he mean? I had never even met him before. I hardly came to Dubai since we did not even have an office there.

'I didn't get your name, sir. May I know your name, please?' I asked.

His laugh was bittersweet. He said, 'I am Portado, your classmate.'

I was very happy to see him and shook his hand. 'Oh, Portado, I am seeing you after thirty-five years! It has been so long that I didn't recognize you. Physically, both of us have changed so much. It is nice to meet you. Stay back. If you are here, come for dinner tonight. I want to catch up,' I said.

Sadly, Portado said, 'Sorry, I don't have much time. I am in the night shift. But I can have a cup of tea with you.'

We went to the hotel restaurant and I ordered a cup

of tea for him and juice for myself. I wanted to talk more. I started the conversation with great enthusiasm and could not hold my questions back. 'Portado, where are you working now? How long have you been in Dubai? Are you married? How many children do you have? By the way, how are your networking friends? Do you ever come to India?'

Portado stopped me. 'I know your work involves computers but mine does not. You are too fast for me. Just like a computer. But I am in construction. So bear with me since I am slow. I have been in Dubai for the last five years. Before that, I was in India in several small places in different companies. Of course, I am married. I have two daughters.'

I interrupted him. 'You could have brought them today. I would have liked to meet them.'

'Sorry, I can't bring them because they are not here. I am in the lower level of management. So I cannot afford to bring my family here. My two daughters are studying in India and are doing engineering. I can't even afford their education in this place.'

I did not know what to say. I had never imagined Portado would end up like this.

Now it was his turn to talk. 'Do you remember, when I was in college, I used to make fun of all of you? I spent all my time in networking. After I finished engineering, I didn't get a good job. The reason was very obvious. I did not have the knowledge or the ability to work hard. I looked down upon the two qualities that are the stepping stones to success. I knew that I wanted to go up and reach the top spot in a company but no one can just fly there. I knew what position I should be in but I did not know the route. I thought that a change of job will help, but instead it reduced my value in the market. None of my networking friends helped me. They dropped me like a hot potato. They thought that I was clinging on to them like a parasite. Some of them were like me and also looking for jobs. I always thought that I would come up with someone's help. I never thought that I should take my own help. Now I am old. I am trying to learn new things and make up for lost time. But it is not easy. The market has become extremely competitive. Youngsters in college have more knowledge and quickness. They also have time on their side. I have told my daughters, you should study, get knowledge, learn skills and work hard.'

Portado continued, 'Do you remember who said this to me? It was you.'

He looked at his watch and said, 'My time is up. I must leave.'

I wished him all the best.

He walked a few steps, then came back and said, 'That day, I called you a nerd. Today, I call you smart.'

And he left.

19

Uncle Sam

Our village was thirty kilometres away from the main city. So many people like Keshav lived in our village and commuted to the city, which worked out cheaper. Keshav was our neighbour and he worked for a private company in the city.

Keshav had two sons. One of them went to New York and started working there. The other one became a college lecturer in the city. Keshav was very proud of his son in America. In the sixties and seventies, it was a great achievement to go to America. The possibility of a better future in India was bleak. The jobs offered were either in the government or in public sector companies. Our government strongly discouraged any entrepreneurial activity. The dividends were charged taxes of 98 per cent and imported goods were very expensive. Even now, I clearly remember that when my father booked a Fiat car, the waiting period was seventeen years! Having a telephone at home was also a rich man's affair. The government policies were so strict that it made foreign travel next to impossible, even for wealthy people. In those days, whenever somebody went abroad, even to a place nearby like Bangkok, Hong Kong or Singapore, people would say 'Bon Voyage' in a special section of the local newspaper to spread the word in the city and inform the relatives. When they returned, their picture was printed in the newspaper to announce the successful completion of their tour.

In such an economic situation, Keshav's older son, Mahesh, went on a scholarship to the USA and settled there. The percentage of people who went on a student visa and returned to India was hardly one per cent and Mahesh was no exception to the rule. He was probably the first person from our village to go to the USA. Keshav spoke proudly of him. He fondly referred to him as 'my son in New York' rather than as Mahesh. Whenever anyone went to his house, they saw lots of photographs of Mahesh—in colour, which was rare back then. The different pictures showed Mahesh and his wife standing in front of their car or visiting Niagara Falls or the Statue of Liberty dressed in winter coats with snow all around them.

Whenever Mahesh came to India, he brought two heavy suitcases containing perfumes, cigarette lighters, nylon saris, suit pieces, plastic lunch boxes, cigarettes and many other things. He displayed all of them in his parents' living room. Most people in our village went to meet him to ask about life in America. He talked about life there as if it was a fairyland. 'I stay in a small town near New York. The roads are so clean and neat; there is not an inch of dust there. We don't lock our houses. Nobody comes and steals anything from anyone. When you go to a departmental store there, you get various juices like orange, grape and musambi. They are sold in huge glass jars and we don't have to return the jars. At the billing counter, the items are given in a plastic bag and it is not even charged. You can get everything under one roof, unlike in India. The grocery stores there contain a variety of food which you can't even imagine.' Then Mahesh would show some photographs of the grocery stores.

His brother's wife, Rama, served tea or coffee to the visitors. But Mahesh's wife, Malathi, sat with her husband and continued his speech from where he left off.

'Whenever I wear a sari and go out, people look at me and tell me how beautiful I am. They touch my silk sari and ask me many questions about how I drape it so beautifully. They also look at my bindi and ask many questions. Cooking is a joy there. You get cut and frozen vegetables. If you go to the Indian store, we get the best curry ingredients, and you can't get that quality in India. The best quality is sent there as export. Just the other day, I saw *elaichi* in Rama's kitchen. It was so small. But look at the elaichi that I have brought from there. They are ten times bigger.'

Normally, Mahesh gave a small gift to everybody who visited him—a bottle of perfume, a pack of cigarettes, a sachet of Spanish saffron or cinnamon sticks. It was a custom in our village that when you received a gift, you had to reciprocate. So people requested Mahesh and his family to come to their house for tea or dinner. Mahesh would turn to his wife and ask her, 'Dear, are we free that day? Shall we accept this invite?' Malathi would pull out an appointment diary, make a fuss and say, 'So sorry, we are not free that day.' We had never heard the word 'dear' being used in our village before. We considered it very awkward to call a wife 'dear' in public. But Mahesh would explain, 'That's how a husband and wife address each other in America.'

Mahesh and Malathi had two children—a boy and a girl. They wore beautiful clothes and went around the village wearing imported shoes. Malathi always told her children, 'Don't drink water in anybody's house. Don't eat raw salads here either. Be careful of the mosquito bites and wear a hat so that you don't get sunburnt.'

Rama used to get tired of Malathi's stay in the village. While Keshav and his wife enjoyed the company of 'their son and daughter-in-law from New York', she had to do all the work. Malathi did not like to help because she said that there was so much dirt here. Rama had to boil water and make different dishes every day, according to Mahesh and his family's demands.

Many years passed. Our joint family no longer remained joint. The ancestral home no longer existed. I still referred to our uncles, aunts and cousins as family but the truth was that the relationship was less like one between family members and more like that between acquaintances. Our entire family was spread out in different parts of India and the globe. Physically, there was a distance separating us. In our minds, there was a larger distance between us. And even worse, in our hearts, there was a great chasm that divided us.

The other day, I was surprised to meet Mahesh in the city. Now he looked fit and energetic but somewhere I felt I saw sadness in his eyes. I was very happy to see him after so long. I asked him, 'Do you have time for a cup of tea?'

Without referring to the appointment diary, he

immediately agreed. We went to a nearby cafe and started chatting. 'When did you come here? How is Malathi Akka? How are your children? I heard that they have done very well at studies.'

'I came a few days ago. Malathi has gone to Mount Abu. The children are busy as usual.'

'Is Malathi Akka on a holiday without you?' At the back of my mind, I remembered the word 'dear' which I had heard for the first time when I was a teenager.

'No. She has joined the Brahma Kumaris. They run a successful branch in America. Malathi is in charge of one centre. I find that there is so much change in India.'

'Of course, India has changed a lot in the last two decades.' I asked again, 'Where are your children?'

'My daughter did her MBA from Harvard. She is now in the West Coast, married to a Chinese man and happily settled. My son is pursuing his thesis on "The Difficulties of African Tribes" at New York City and right now he is in Zimbabwe.'

'How is your brother Ramesh? What about his family? I hardly go to the village now. So I don't know how people are doing. After your father's death, we hardly hear about your family.'

'Ramesh is doing exceedingly well. When we were young, he bought a patch of land in the outskirts of the village. We all thought that it was a bad investment and that he should have bought the land adjacent to the highway. But today, there are bridges, underpasses and further expansion of the roads. The government has taken all the land on either side of the highway. Our village is no longer remote. It is an extension of the city. Ramesh has converted his land to a resort and makes good money out of it. His son runs the business and even owns a petrol bunk. Our ancestral home is converted to a shopping mall, and I sold my share of the property to Ramesh for a few thousand rupees in those days. Hmm. There are many things that I shouldn't have done.'

I saw a distinct expression of regret on his face. I was curious to know more but I did not ask. I thought that if he wanted to share, I would let him do so in his own time.

Mahesh continued, 'There is nothing to hide. The Government of India has opened up many opportunities with its new policy in 1991 and hence there are tremendous job prospects in India. I can feel India vibrating with the economic boom and high energy. I find that there is at least one person abroad from each family in our village now. It is no longer a novelty to go to America. Whatever we get there, we can buy in India at a much cheaper price. The land prices have gone up so much that it is more expensive to buy property in India than in the US. Ramesh is the best example of this. I made a mistake.'

'What do you mean?'

'I should not have gone to Uncle Sam's land.'

20

You Should Have Asked Me

I have known Rakesh for a long time. A few years ago, he called me up and said, 'You know that we manufacture school bags in our factory. There are always seconds with small defects. We can probably sell them for half the price depending on the defect. But I thought that it is better to give them to you for free because you can at least distribute them to needy children in rural areas. Will you come once a year and collect the bags from us?'

I was absolutely thrilled by his offer because it is hard to get such donations for rural schools. Most wealthy people live in big cities and if they donate money, it is usually in the city itself. There are a few people who give back to their hometowns but hardly anyone ever gives to rural areas that they are not connected to. Sometimes,

I feel that villages and towns are benefited only if a rich philanthropist originates from that area. Otherwise, thousands of villages go unnoticed without anyone's help and remain totally dependent on the government. I work in such villages where a small donation can make a big difference to its children. Rakesh's offer was like chancing upon a gold mine.

'Rakesh, thank you so much for your help,' I said. 'If you want, I will give you the list of schools where we will distribute your bags. Do you need a letter from us?'

He gave a hearty laugh and said, 'Oh, there is absolutely no formality. You don't have to inform me about anything. I have faith and trust in you. You can come and collect the bags every year in May before the school year starts.'

It is very difficult to earn trust. It takes years to build and it can be destroyed in an instant by one bad deed. Trust requires an enormous amount of integrity and you have to prove every time that you are worthy of it. I am very grateful to our society and community. The Infosys Foundation has built a great reputation for itself and everybody is ready to help us with anything that we might need.

Every year, my assistant went and met the factory manager, and he would bring the bags back with him.

After a few months, my assistant said, 'Ma'am, there is a new manager in the factory.' So I had to explain the whole process to the new manager, which took some time. These days, it is hard to retain employees in any company. So I decided to send an email to the new manager explaining the process and for recordkeeping. The new manager acknowledged my email and the yearly visits to collect the bags went on. In the last ten years, there were four new factory managers but the procedure always remained the same.

Meanwhile, Rakesh grew old. He decided to retire and move back to Delhi. One day, he called me and said, 'I am shifting base to Delhi. Bharat, my son-in-law, will now run this office. I have explained the process to him. So he is aware of the annual donation and you don't have to worry. Nothing is going to change.'

I thanked him and wished him a good retired life.

Bharat joined the factory in April as the new manager. I sent him an email to congratulate him and to explain the usual process. I did not get a reply.

My assistant went to the factory in May that year. All the bags were packed and loaded in the truck. Then Bharat called my assistant and said, 'Please don't load the truck until your chairperson comes and meets me. Kindly unload the truck if you have already loaded it.'

My assistant sent the message to me quickly. As I was the receiver, it was my duty to go meet the donor. I cleared my schedule and went and met Bharat the next day. He said, 'How can you take goods without informing me?'

'Sir, I sent you an email when you joined the factory,' I said. 'Whenever there is a change in management, we have always sent an email explaining the practice. We have had the same procedure for the last ten years. The process was set up by Rakesh. Is there anything wrong?'

'If Rakesh sir started it, I don't have any objections. But I am a new person. Is it not your duty to come and meet me? After all, this is a gift. So it cannot go out without my permission. I haven't received your email at all. It was a shock for me to see your team pack up the seconds and take them away.'

I said, 'That is not true. You can see it in the logs of previous years. We take the seconds once a year in May and also send a thank-you letter to your company.'

'We will send the goods as soon as I receive an email from you,' he said.

I replied, 'But we have already sent an email.'

Bharat argued, 'Maybe, but I haven't received it. You can resend it.'

I came back to my office and was wondering about

the real reason behind this unpleasantness. I checked my email and saw that I had received a read receipt of the email that I had sent Bharat. That meant Bharat had seen my email and was lying to me. Still, I resent the email.

As I sat at my desk, I thought about what had happened. I realized that the email was not the issue. It was Bharat's ego. He was upset because I did not go to meet him as soon as he became the new manager. He thought that the best way to show his importance was to call and tell me that I could not take the seconds without his permission. Now I understood. I was not upset at all. If someone wants me to satisfy their ego by going and standing in front of them in person, I can do so for the sake of the poor children. If I did not go, I would not hurt myself but I would hurt the poor children.

Every human being has an ego. But it is up to us to decide how much we have and how we exercise it. Rakesh's son-in-law was young and had less life experience than Rakesh or me. I could have called Rakesh and told him about what was going on. However, I did not want this to become an issue and cause a fight in the family. But I knew that Bharat would definitely give me the bags in the end.

The next morning, I got a call. 'Madam, I received your email just now. Your assistant can come and collect the bags.' Bharat never used the word 'sorry' even though I was older than him.

'Sorry, Bharat, for the miscommunication,' I said. 'Going forward, every May, we will send you a physical letter. Also, after receiving the school bags, we will send you another letter thanking you. Is that okay? Is there anything else we can do to improve communication? Please let me know. We are ready to make changes.'

There was a pause on the other end. I took another breath and said, 'Can you hear me?'

'Yes, madam. We trust you. We don't need any letters.'

I kept the phone down and smiled. A fire cannot be extinguished with another fire. It is only water that can make a difference.

21

A Mother's Love

Mahanadi is a big river in Odisha and it is breathtaking to see the river in December. But if you want to see her anger, you should take an appointment with her in June, during the rainy season. Her colour is reddish-brown then and the river overflows every year. The poor people who live on the banks have to vacate their homes. The Mahanadi floods have become so common that rehabilitation is a mandatory agenda in Odisha's budget.

We were working in one of these flood-relief areas near Paradweep. The Infosys Foundation supports an orphanage meant for mentally and physically challenged children there.

When I arrived in Bhubaneswar, our Foundation team leader said, 'Let's leave immediately for the spot.'

I said, 'Don't be in a hurry. On the first day of such

a disaster, more than victims, there are people such as newspaper reporters, TV crew, social workers and government officers hanging about. In the middle of this chaos, the progress of the relief work is very slow. There are already people there who are being rescued. We will go tomorrow. By that time, we will know what they have already received and what they really need. We should be prepared to look after ourselves with water and basic amenities and we must also carry vaccinations.'

When we started the next day, I said, 'Let's take a jeep or minivan so that we can bring the children back. Please keep some quilts, biscuits and water bottles ready.'

My new assistant, Varun, asked, 'What do you mean?'

I replied, 'If we find some children, we have to bring them back and put them in the special needs children's school.'

'How do you know that you will get such children?'

'From my experience.'

He was genuinely puzzled. I explained, 'During floods, poor people have to run away in minimum time with the maximum goods that are an asset to them. They take their clothes and money along with their healthy children. If they have challenged children, they leave them behind. So, in the course of relief work, we find such children and put them in the special needs residential school nearby. Sometimes, parents come back and take their children home. But sometimes, they don't.'

'How can you talk like this, madam?' asked Varun, visibly shocked.

'Try to understand the situation, Varun. If they don't have any vehicle and they have to wait for these challenged children to come with them, they will lose everything including their own lives. It is not that they don't love their children, but the extreme economic situation forces them to leave them behind. Be sympathetic to them.'

'I don't agree with you, madam. A mother's love is the highest and most unconditional love in the world. She will sacrifice everything for her children.'

'That may be true often, Varun, but don't generalize about it,' I said.

We all went to work. When we came back that day, we had found four such children.

That night, when we assembled, Varun asked me, 'Madam, I am still confused about a mother's love for her children. You must have worked in many places. Tell me your thoughts about this topic.'

I said, 'Come, sit next to me. I will share a few stories with you.'

I began, 'One day, I read a very funny report about

how a mother chimpanzee behaves in adversity. This experiment was conducted a few years ago. A mother and a baby chimpanzee were kept in a big, empty and transparent glass tank with a closed glass ceiling. They were playing happily. After some time, the researchers started filling the tank with water. As the water level started increasing, the mother chimpanzee became alert, held the baby to her heart and started standing up and howling. She was upset and wanted to break the glass ceiling. Still, the water level continued to rise. She changed her position and kept the baby on one of her shoulders. Then, she kept moving the baby from one shoulder to another. But when the water level came up to her nose, she put the baby below her feet and tried to climb on the baby so that she could breathe. At this point, the researchers drained the water out. This experiment clearly shows that everyone loves his or her life more than anyone else's. I was surprised by how any mother could do this. I reasoned that this may be true only for chimpanzees and may not be true for humans because, after all, we are more social animals and more culturally aware, or at least I hope so.'

Varun said, 'That is so interesting, madam. Tell me more.'

I continued, 'This next story is about Chatrapati Shivaji's era. He was a great warrior, had extraordinary abilities and was a true patriot.

'There was a young married woman called Hirakani who lived in a village near Raigarh, one of Shivaji's forts. She was a milkmaid and supplied milk and milk products to the fort every day. The main door of the fort was known as Simha Dwaram and it was open from sunrise to sunset.

'After some time, Hirakani gave birth to a baby. Every day, she continued to go to Shivaji's fort and supply milk. She returned home before sunset because the gates of the fort closed at sunset and nobody was allowed to enter or leave the fort unless they took permission from the king himself.

'One day, a soldier's wife was in labour inside the fort and Hirakani went to help her. By the time the baby was born, it was night and the doors had been closed. She begged the security guards at the fort gates to open a small slit so that she could go home and take care of her baby who had to be breastfed. There was nobody in the house to take care of the baby. She cried and cried but, even though they felt bad, the guards were afraid to open the doors because it was against the king's orders.

'Then Hirakani thought of an alternative way to reach her baby. The only other way to go home was to climb the hill and jump from there. She knew that she might survive because there was a meadow below with a stream. But she might also die or break her legs. But her motherly instincts did not allow her to sit quietly and do nothing.

'Hirakani prayed to God and, gathering all her courage, she jumped. Luckily, she fell on a treetop and was able to climb down. Then, she went home, bruised but not badly injured.

'The next morning, she carried milk and curd and entered the fort as usual. The guards were surprised to see her. They thought that she was already inside. They asked Hirakani, "How did you reach home safe and sound?"

'She told them the whole episode. Then, she said, "The need of my child is more important than my life. After all, I am a mother. For a mother, the child is an extension of her body. No mother can live in peace when she knows that her child is in danger."

'She walked away as if nothing had happened.

'Soon, news spread that there was a way to escape from the formidable fort, which worried Shivaji. But he knew that even the greatest warrior would think twice before jumping from the hilltop.

'He called Hirakani and honoured her. He told her, "You have a great *matra hridaya*." In her honour, one of the *burjs* of the fort was named Hirakani and it lasts even today.'

I stopped and looked at Varun. 'So, Varun, don't generalize about anything,' I said. 'Decisions are taken depending on the circumstances, but still, I believe that a mother's love is the most unconditional in the world.'

22

Do You Remember?

Dr Raj Reddy, a professor at Carnegie Mellon, won the Alan Turing Award in 1994 for his pioneering efforts in computer science and artificial intelligence. This award is highly coveted and is equivalent to a Nobel Prize in computer science. He was the first person of Asian origin to win this award.

I was very happy that an Indian had received such a prestigious award. I came to know that Dr Reddy was in Bangalore and went to congratulate him.

Went I entered his house, I saw lots of bouquets and gifts scattered around the living room. It was obvious that many people had been visiting him. He was resting in his armchair and wore white cotton pants and a shirt. He was so simply dressed that one could never have guessed that he was such a distinguished person. His wife was busy inside the kitchen preparing snacks.

I thought that Dr Reddy must be really excited about his super success. I said, 'You must be feeling right on top of the world. It is a great milestone to receive this award and it is a big achievement. Don't you feel proud?'

Instead of answering, he smiled at me affectionately. He seemed very calm and peaceful. He said, 'I want to ask you some questions.'

I was so surprised that I almost fell off my chair. I said, 'Sure, sir.'

'Do you remember who got the Nobel Prize in Chemistry last year?'

Though I read the paper every day, I could not recollect the name. 'I don't remember who got the prize for chemistry but I can tell you who got the Nobel Prize for Peace or in Literature in the last two or three years,' I said.

He laughed, 'Peace and literature are often controversial because of their subjective nature. So they are always highlighted in the news. No, I want to know about chemistry.'

I accepted my defeat.

Then he asked me, 'Do you know who was elected Fellow of the Royal Society in London last year?'

Again, I was at a loss.

He asked me another question, 'Do you remember who got the Pulitzer Prize this year?'

'No. But I know the shortlist for the Booker Prize. One of them was Romesh Gunesekera.'

'You remember his name because he is an Asian too.'

'The answer to all your questions can be found on the Internet. I am growing old and I don't remember a lot of things these days,' I defended myself.

He smiled at me again. 'My intention is not to test your memory. It is just to tell you that nobody remembers all the prizewinners all the time. People remember the achievers in their own field or if they are close relatives or friends. The rest of the world reads your name in the newspapers and forgets easily. And that is the right thing to do. So, whenever I get a prize, I always know that only some people will remember this and that too for only a short time. There is nothing great about it. My prize is that I have enjoyed my work. When I win awards, there are some genuine people who share this joy with me. To me, that is the greatest honour.'

His attitude really impressed me. He was not overjoyed when he received an award, nor was he sad when he did not get one. Such people are rare in life. That is the reason I will always respect and remember Dr Raj Reddy.

He asked me in a lighter mood, 'I want to ask you one more thing. Do you remember people who have made a lasting impression on you?'

Within a fraction of a second, I replied, 'Oh, I remember my kindergarten teacher. When my mother left me on the first day at school, I started crying. My teacher came and hugged me and said, "Baby, don't worry. Don't get scared. I am with you." At that age, it was so encouraging that someone was with me in a strange school. I remember my classmate too. I had broken a neighbour's window while playing and was too scared to tell my parents. She said, "Don't worry. I will come with you and tell your parents that we both did it." I also remember one of my cousins. My bus was delayed and I reached her home at midnight. Still, my cousin woke up and cooked an awesome meal for me without an inch of dissatisfaction. I even remember my teacher who scolded me when I didn't do my homework in time. He said, "Time is precious. If you don't do your work on time, it is as good as not doing it." His scolding changed my life forever.'

Dr Raj Reddy smiled and said, 'See, those are the important things in life. Those people might not have achieved anything in the eyes of the world. But they made you secure and confident. They made you feel like a rock star. They gave you strength, courage and values. They are the true prizes in your life and you should always cherish them.'

23

Life's Secret Lessons

It was 1996. I knew that India had twenty-five states and seven union territories and that a majority of us spoke a total of thirty languages. Each state had its own culture, tradition, dress code and folk art. I was aware of the great sages and writers of the land and knew the names of most mountains and rivers of our country.

That was my India as I knew it.

After joining Infosys Foundation that year, I learnt that my perception of India was not India at all. My perception was only a statistical description of India. I realized that there is so much helplessness and poverty here. Poverty does not mean just a lack of money but also a lack of confidence. Money can be earned in life but confidence is easy to lose and very hard to gain back. I learnt lessons that no book could ever teach me and no Internet site could show me, because I had access to real people. Very few people have this privilege.

Still, I usually never know the real opinion of most people I converse with. The reason is that people whom I do not give money to criticize me and people who hope to receive money from me say that I am great. So I have made many enemies and only a few true friends. Now I understand why people at the top are always lonely.

My First Lesson

At times, I feel that only children tell the truth and are the real judges of one's talent. Once I was in Calcutta for the launch of a children's book. Children from various schools came and attended the event. As a part of the book launch, I had to read a few stories from my book. When I started reading, a young boy got up and innocently said, 'Aunty, you write well, but you don't read well.'

I looked at him. He was around twelve years old and had intelligent and sharp eyes. His teacher was about to hush him when I stopped her, 'Please allow him to speak. Children are unbiased and clear in their thinking. They say the truth and the truth alone. Maybe the passage of time changes them. But for now, let him say whatever he wants to say.'

Then I called the boy to me. I asked him, 'Can you read the story for me?'

'Of course, I can read it. I am an actor in my school and I know how to modulate the voice which you don't do.'

'I agree. I am not an actress. I am only a writer.'

The child read the entire story with different modulations and I was quite impressed. I felt that I was meeting a genuine critic of my readings for the first time.

That was my first lesson.

My Second Lesson

As part of my work for the Foundation, I travelled the corners of India, which I would not have done otherwise. Our team worked through five national natural disasters like the earthquake in Gujarat, the tsunami in Tamil Nadu and the Andamans, the drought in Maharashtra and Karnataka, floods in Odisha, Karnataka and Andhra Pradesh and hurricanes in Odisha.

Every disaster taught me my second lesson. I learnt that there is a limitation to human power and achievements, and that even with money you cannot help everyone. You cannot substitute many things in life with money.

My Third Lesson

As I worked with the Foundation, my horizons changed. I met the poorest of the poor, the most talented artists, the victims of natural disasters and the most successful people who climbed the ladder with their hard work. I saw many ungrateful receivers as well. All of them became part of my big canvas. The amazing thing I saw was that, most times, what people presented outside was never how it was inside. The moment you went near, their carefully constructed image started falling apart.

When someone cheated me, I got upset and angry. I usually called that person and scolded him or her. I expressed my anger and disappointment to them. Even now, I remember many experiences of children cheating parents, and vice versa. It was very disillusioning.

A few years ago at the Foundation, we reserved Monday mornings to give money to poor people to buy medicines for cancer treatment. These people usually brought letters from cancer hospitals.

One day, my car was near the entrance gate of our Foundation. I was waiting in the car for an umbrella since it had started raining. I looked around and noticed a car in front of me. A lady was sitting in the backseat of the car. I saw her remove her diamond earrings and then she got down from the car. I did not think much of it at the time. Soon I got my umbrella and went to my office. There I saw the same lady with a letter asking us for some cancer medicine. If the incident had happened ten years ago, I would have given her a piece of my mind. But now, I smiled at her and told her gently, 'Sorry, madam. We can't give money to you. Cancer medicines are much cheaper than diamond earrings. There are many people who require this free medicine more than you.'

Now I look at life differently. Most people do not have the same values when they get money. Money changes a person completely. Very few people can withstand the lure of money and they are difficult to find. I have learnt that wherever there is money, people like to take advantage of the situation and maximize their return.

My Fourth Lesson

I have also received many life lessons from the poorest of the poor.

On one of my trips, I was visiting a village. It was late evening and I stayed with a friend, Neerav, who had a big house. His late grandfather was a well-known local language writer who had achieved great laurels during his lifetime. His grandmother kept talking about him and his awards. Neerav took me aside and said, 'Sorry, my grandmother lives in the past. She does not understand that today many people have forgotten my grandfather even though he was a hero in the old days.'

I asked him, 'Will you show me the room with the awards that your grandmother described?'

He took me upstairs and opened a room full of dust. Of course, there were many awards there, citations and medals. There was also a box full of shawls, and countless dusty volumes. He said, 'When my grandfather was alive, people used to visit him all the time. All his colleagues are dead now. We have hundreds of photographs but we don't recognize a single person in them. We have so many books and grandmother doesn't even want to give them to a library. We don't know what to do with his awards. We can't keep them and neither can we throw them away. I live in Mumbai and have a small two-bedroom apartment. My children occupy one room and we occupy the other. I am the only heir to the family. Grandmother insists that I keep all these things; but I have realized that when a person passes away, what he may have collected materially over a period of time becomes irrelevant to the next generation. I can only keep one photograph of my grandfather. And maybe one of his books, as a memento. My children can't even read and write our native language, even though they can speak it fluently. So his whole library is of no use to me. If my grandmother had allowed me to donate these books immediately after my grandfather's death, at least some people from his generation would have read them. Now these books are useless.'

Suddenly, I realized that this was my next lesson. If we keep collecting material things, it becomes a burden to the next generation. It is better that we reduce our cache while we are alive. This was a great message and I started practising it. Today, I immediately give away what I do not need.

My Fifth Lesson

During one of my train journeys, I met a lady. She hugged me and held my hand tightly. Then she sat next to me and said, 'Oh, don't you remember me? I am your classmate from Hubli. You used to share my lunch with me every day. I have read all your books.'

I was very uncomfortable because I did not remember her and she was not letting go of my hand. But I thought that sometimes it is hard to recognize a person because of changes in external appearance due to age and passage of time.

I told her, 'I am sorry. I don't remember you. However, it is nice to meet you.'

The lady still would not leave me. At the end, she gave me a letter. She said, 'My son is very intelligent and is going abroad for further studies. Can the Foundation help him?'

This behaviour was not an exception because I receive such requests all the time. I have met many people who want to take advantage of the Foundation's name and my position in it. I have learnt that whenever I meet a person, I should expect to get a letter from him or her soon asking for money. All of them remind me that I am like a water tap in a dry area—unthanked if it runs and cursed if it doesn't. I have learnt to be patient and to recognize people's intentions.

My Sixth Lesson

I was attending a music concert and I sat at the back because I thought that I could easily leave if I get bored. There were two well-dressed women wearing big diamond earrings sitting in front of me. Let's call the first lady A and the second one B. I could see that they were from affluent families. They were quite loud in their conversation. So I could clearly hear what they were saying.

A said to B, 'My daughter is quite useless. I want her to work somewhere. Then it will be easy to say in the matrimonial market that she is working. But I don't know who would employ her.'

B replied, 'Oh, don't worry. Get her into teaching.'

A said, 'Oh, she tried. But the school sent her back.'

They must have been best friends or sisters confiding in each other. A was behaving as if she was the student and B was the teacher.

'Then tell her to start an NGO.'

'Isn't it hard to start an NGO and work for it?' asked A with great concern.

B confidently replied, 'It is the easiest job in the world. I will give you an example. Look at Sudha Murty. She doesn't have the brains and is not even talented. So she runs an NGO and has even made a name for herself. When she can run an NGO, anybody can run one.'

I had to interrupt their conversation. So I tapped one of them on the shoulder.

'Do you know Sudha Murty?' I asked.

Confidently, B said, 'Of course.' A seemed baffled but B looked confident. 'Of course, we know her very well.'

'When did you last meet her?'

'This morning—and by the way, who are you?'

Calmly, I replied, 'I am Sudha Murty.'

Without batting an eyelid, B gave me a big smile and said, 'Oh, you have changed so much since morning. I didn't even recognize you.'

'No, I haven't changed,' I said, 'because I never met you in the morning. I want to give you some unsolicited advice, because I really feel that you need it. When a doctor makes a mistake, a person goes six feet below the ground. When a judge makes a mistake, a person is hung six feet above the ground. But when a teacher makes a mistake, the entire batch of students is destroyed. Don't ever look down on teachers. If you had good teachers, you wouldn't be sitting here talking like this today. Don't look down on social work either. Only a person with a compassionate heart and sound judgement can be a philanthropist. When a person in front of you is in need of help, you must decide in a short duration whether you should give money to that person or not, how much you should give and for how long. Understanding human beings is much more difficult than understanding computers. I will accept that I may not be intelligent but, more than that, you should know that you are stupid.'

I walked out feeling brave and happy.

From this incident, I learnt that I must always stand up for myself and follow my heart, even if other people do not always agree with me or like it.

My Seventh Lesson

My son, Rohan, taught me the most important lesson about public speaking.

He said, 'Amma, whenever you are on stage and are giving a speech, please remember that most people are not listening to you. Don't be under the false impression that they have come to listen to you talking about your valuable experiences. They have come to see you because you are a well-known personality, a writer and, more important, it is very hard to meet you in real life. Most of the time you are touring and if you are in office, there are hurdles like security and personal assistants. They won't allow just anyone to come and see you. The Foundation is not run on your personal money. It is corporate money and it's like a honey pot. Wherever there is honey, human beings, ants and honeybees either want to suck it or hoard it for themselves. You are usually not guarded on stage. It is easy for people to give their applications directly to you. That is why they come to see you. Don't let it go to your head.'

I realized the value of this lesson and it has helped in keeping me balanced and grounded.

Usually, I plug my ears when people exaggerate my qualities. I know what I am and I know my shortcomings.

In the twelfth century, there was a famous poetess, Akka Mahadevi, who prayed to God and said, 'Please make me deaf. That way, I won't hear other sounds and can concentrate only on you.' I follow her. So I switch my mind off during introduction sessions.

Once I went to a function as a speaker and there were many important men and women on the stage with me. I mentally switched off as the introductions started. After some time, I heard everyone clapping. I thought that it would be bad manners not to clap and I clapped along with everybody. The person sitting next to me looked at me a bit funnily. I tried to focus on what was being said. The speaker was saying that the lady he was introducing had extraordinary qualities that only Goddess Saraswati could match. He continued praising the lady so I asked the person sitting next to me, 'Do you know who he is talking about? Which of the speakers has these qualities? I don't think I have ever met anyone like her. Have you met her?'

He looked at me kindly and said, 'He is talking about you.'

I was really upset but I knew how to express my discomfort. When it was my turn to speak, I said, 'Please discount my introduction. I am a very ordinary person and I am only here because situations and circumstances have led me here. I am just like any one of you.'

But it did not really matter what I said, because Rohan was right. I still received fifty applications that day.

My Eighth Lesson

In 2005, I was in South Africa. I hired a taxi and decided to see the tourist spots in Cape Town. My cab driver was a friendly white man. He started talking to me as we travelled together.

'Ma'am, my name is John. Are you from India?'

I was more interested in looking outside the window of our moving car. So, I said briefly, 'Yes, I am.'

'Are you enjoying your visit to our country?'

I said, 'Of course. I am a big fan of history and there is so much to be learnt here. I feel like an excited explorer. South Africa is home to famous Nobel laureates such as Nelson Mandela and Desmond Tutu. I am really happy to be here.'

'Ma'am, apart from great laureates, we are also home to other great leaders. There are leaders in South Africa who never won a medal or a prize, but they have left behind a legacy for thousands of years to come. My favourite is Mahatma Gandhi.'

That perked my interest. I was baffled and curious at the same time. Mahatma Gandhi was a leader of my country, not South Africa. How could he say such a thing? I replied, 'John, Mahatma Gandhi is Indian. He is the greatest leader of our country. I don't mean to start a debate here but he is not South African at all. He spent a few years in South Africa during his lifetime but that doesn't make him South African.'

John started smiling. 'Ma'am, when he came here, he was M.K. Gandhi. But he went back as Mahatma Gandhi. He learnt about the non-cooperative movement and the goodness of non-violence here. This became a fundamental tool of freedom struggle in your country. He didn't just transform your country. He changed ours too. He is remembered and highly respected in South Africa. He is a world leader.'

I had to agree. 'You are right, John,' I said. 'I never thought of it that way. I always considered him to be the Father of our Nation. But I know that he never considered himself to be only a part of one nation. He wanted to make a difference to the world.'

I learnt that when a person becomes a compassionate leader like Mahatma Gandhi, Gautam Buddha, Martin Luther King Jr or Abraham Lincoln, they do not just belong to one country. They transcend man-made boundaries and are recognized as leaders of the world.